Academic Careers
and the Gender Gap

Academic Careers and the Gender Gap

MAUREEN BAKER

UBCPress · Vancouver · Toronto

21 20 19 18 17 16 15 14 13 12   5 4 3 2 1

Printed in Canada on FSC-certified ancient-forest-free paper
(100% post-consumer recycled) that is processed chlorine- and acid-free.

Library and Archives Canada Cataloguing in Publication

Baker, Maureen
   Academic careers and the gender gap / Maureen Baker.

Includes bibliographical references and index.
Issued also in electronic formats.
ISBN 978-0-7748-2396-8 (bound); ISBN 978-0-7748-2397-5 (pbk.)

   1. Women college teachers. 2. Women in higher education. 3. Work and family.
4. Sex role in the work environment. 5. Universities and colleges – Social aspects. I. Title.

| LB2332.3.B34 2012 | 378.1'2082 | C2012-903440-1 |

Canadä

UBC Press gratefully acknowledges the financial support for our publishing program of the Government of Canada (through the Canada Book Fund), the Canada Council for the Arts, and the British Columbia Arts Council.

This book has been published with the help of a grant from the Canadian Federation for the Humanities and Social Sciences, through the Awards to Scholarly Publications Program, using funds provided by the Social Sciences and Humanities Research Council of Canada.

UBC Press
The University of British Columbia
2029 West Mall
Vancouver, BC V6T 1Z2
www.ubcpress.ca

Contents

Tables

Preface and Acknowledgments

This book arose from four decades of scholarly interest in gendered patterns of work and more specifically in university-based academic work. In the late 1960s, as an undergraduate student at the University of Toronto, I discovered that Canadian men with eight years of elementary school education earned more money than women with a master's degree. This correlation, which I found in a Statistics Canada publication in my college library, inspired me to continue my formal education to the highest level. When I began my doctorate at the University of Alberta in 1972, there were no women in tenure-track positions in the Sociology Department. I thought I wanted to become a university professor but had few female role models, which encouraged me to study academic women for my doctoral research. In 2008, as a senior professor working in New Zealand, I decided to re-examine the academic gender gap by interviewing academic men and women in two different types of universities in that country. This book includes both of these studies, based on qualitative interviews from 1973 and 2008, as well as an extensive survey of the research on gender patterns of work, restructuring in academia, and the academic gender gap in the liberal states, including Australia, Canada, New Zealand, the United Kingdom, and the United States.

First, I would like to thank Rosalind Sydie, who is now an emeritus professor at the University of Alberta, for supervising my original research in the early 1970s, and Margrit Eichler from the Ontario Institute for Studies in Education in Toronto for examining it. Second, I want to thank Patrizia Albanese from Ryerson University in Toronto for suggesting at a conference a few years ago that I rekindle my research interests in the academic gender gap after so many years. Third, I would like to acknowledge the assistance of Helen Cox and Christine Todd, who helped with the 2008 study and were postgraduate students at the University of Auckland at the time. Fourth, I want to express my appreciation for the support of the staff at UBC Press, especially Darcy Cullen, Ann Macklem, and Deborah Kerr, and the two anonymous reviewers who provided invaluable comments used in the final draft. Finally, I would like to thank David Tippin from the University of Auckland for his extensive discussions about university restructuring and for his continued support throughout the project.

Academic Careers
and the Gender Gap

Setting the Scene 1

Gender has influenced the kinds of choices that I have made,
or perhaps it's also influenced what I felt might be possible.

– FEMALE LECTURER, NEW ZEALAND, 2008

I've always just assumed that I have enjoyed some advantage or
privilege as a result of being male – you know, in the job market and
maybe even in career advancement – but it's something you just
don't really think about that much.

– MALE SENIOR LECTURER, NEW ZEALAND, 2008

Since I was a doctoral student in the 1970s, women's representation among university students, graduates, and academics has increased dramatically, but the quotes above, which come from my recent research, suggest that gender continues to influence aspirations and work patterns. Throughout this book, I discuss a considerable amount of research that shows that an academic gender gap persists for university-based scholars. Notable differences exist in disciplinary specialization, work location, job security and satisfaction, rank, salary, and career development of male and female academics in Australia, Canada, New Zealand, the

United Kingdom, and the United States.¹ Like many workplaces, universities have restructured in recent years, but have these new priorities actually promoted or counteracted gender equity? How are academic careers influenced by institutional practices, collegial relations, personal lives, and perceptions, and how have these changed over the decades? By investigating gendered lives in a restructuring professional setting, I explore issues that remain central to the sociology of work, gender studies, and the study of personal life.

To better understand how and why the gender gap continues to persist, this book situates academic work within the larger context of changing labour markets, workplace reorganization, and patterns of earning and caring among men and women. Academic work has some unique characteristics compared to other jobs, including its extensive qualifications, its relatively high degree of job control, its international marketplace, and its reliance on entrepreneurial skills for research productivity and promotion. Nevertheless, I argue that it has been influenced by many of the global trends that are visible in other workplaces and that academic employees tend to share patterns of gender relations with wider populations.

This book investigates the ways that the academic gender gap has changed over the decades, how it has been perpetuated, and why this should matter to universities and academics. The topic provides an excellent opportunity to discuss the impact of gender on paid/unpaid work and to highlight the contributions that research on academia can make to sociological and feminist theory. In this volume, the growing body of research on gendered work is integrated with studies of the academic profession, adding findings from two of my own research projects done in different decades and countries. Verbatim quotes from the participants in these two studies are used to illustrate gendered patterns. I analyze structural, relational, and interpretive factors contributing to the academic gender gap, revealing some remarkably similar patterns among five countries.

Despite decades of social change, equity initiatives, and family-friendly policies, I argue that from country to country, the academic gender gap is maintained for much the same reasons. The book focuses on three major areas influencing the gender gap: work-related and institutional matters, typical configurations of family and personal life, and personal ambitions and subjectivities. I present these in three separate chapters as though they are different issues, but they are shown to be closely interconnected. Although I acknowledge that inequalities based on other factors such as ethnicity, culture, race, social class, and a combination of these persist in universities, the tight focus on male/female differences not only contributes to feminist research but also makes the project more manageable when dealing with cross-national comparisons.[2]

Several concepts used throughout the book will be more clearly defined later in this chapter. The first is that of the "liberal states," a term that refers to Australia, Canada, New Zealand, the United Kingdom, and the United States. The second is the "academic gender gap" – the difference between the work-related patterns of men and women faculty, or academic staff.[3] This chapter also briefly explores typical academic practices, university priorities, and restructuring for readers unfamiliar with this environment. In addition, I discuss the focus, methodology, theoretical framework, and main contribution of the book.

Chapter 2 establishes the socio-demographic context behind this analysis of the academic gender gap by providing an overview of labour market trends and gendered patterns of postsecondary education, paid work, and family/personal life in the liberal states. By "gendered patterns" I am referring to differences in the typical trends for men and women, which in the statistics are categorized by biological sex but are actually influenced largely by social constructions of gender and family life. Chapter 3 discusses some of the economic and governance issues underpinning changing university workplaces in the liberal states. Although practices and priorities vary somewhat by university, institutional type, and jurisdiction, I identify a number of significant commonalities that cut across these boundaries, which have also been noted by other researchers (Auriol 2007; Currie, Thiele, and Harris 2002; Fairbrother and Rainnie 2006; Geiger 2004; Mohrman, Ma, and Baker 2008).

I am using the academic profession to explore the ways that professional employees are influenced by institutional priorities and practices, labour market trends, parenthood, and gender, and to draw some conclusions about why the gender gap still exists in universities. In the minds of the general public, academic work typically refers to preparing and delivering lectures to undergraduate students. However, for many scholars it also involves leading seminars for graduate students and supervising and examining their research projects. They may also help to make decisions within their departments and university committees, review manuscripts for scholarly journals and publishers, contribute to their professional associations, and provide expert advice to the greater community. Most importantly for this book, they create and disseminate new knowledge through their own research and publications.

Although many scholars are hired to engage in the three strands of teaching, research, and service, this book focuses on rising expectations of research productivity, as this aspect of university work illustrates a number of global changes over the past four decades.[4] I also concentrate on academics with career-oriented or permanent jobs. These individuals are typically perceived by senior colleagues and managers (such as deans and department heads/chairs) as more successful than doctorates who are employed as long-term part-timers or contingent workers (in temporary positions). However, we need to acknowledge that contingent workers form a growing percentage of academic staff and have become central to both teaching and research (Dobbie and Robinson 2008; Muzzin and Limoges 2008).

After this contextual background, Chapters 4 to 6 present findings from my own interviews with academics in order to investigate more fully the contributors to the academic gender gap. My studies were carried out in two liberal states (Canada and New Zealand), which vary considerably by population but share many similarities in labour market trends, social policies, university restructuring, gendered patterns of paid/unpaid work, family patterns, and gender relations (Baker 2001, 2010b). The fact that the studies were done in differing decades helps to illustrate social and institutional changes over time.

My studies varied somewhat by research design, but both used qualitative interviews to discuss the impact of university priorities, professional expectations, gender, and parenthood on academic careers. Both sets of interviews reveal the subjective experiences of participants and their personal perceptions of academic work, illustrated by their own words. These studies, combined with the wider research, show some enduring patterns but also notable changes since the 1970s.

I conclude in Chapter 7 that the three categories of contributors to the academic gender gap (relating to institutional/professional practices, family/personal life, and subjectivities) are really inseparable and interrelated. This final chapter attempts to distinguish between social constraints (those factors derived from changing work environments, collegial relations, access to social and material support, and gendered home lives) and patterns that reflect beliefs, perceptions, or subjectivities. Some of the sex differences initially appear to be personal choices, but I show that many of these so-called choices are actually shaped by patterns of support and structural limitations. I also argue that similar gendered configurations are apparent in the universities of Australia, Canada, New Zealand, the United Kingdom, and the United States.

The Liberal States and Their Universities
This book draws on studies that investigate changing global labour markets, university practices, and male/female patterns in postsecondary education, paid/unpaid employment, and university-based academic work. First, the analysis focuses on universities alone because colleges and polytechnics have concerns of their own and do not share all the trends apparent in the various categories of universities.

Second, the book focuses on Australia, Canada, New Zealand, the United Kingdom, and the United States because these countries share similar university restructuring processes, patterns of institutional governance, and academic practices. With comparable cultural and policy backgrounds, they also reveal remarkably analogous trends in postsecondary educational attainment of women and men, patterns of paid/unpaid employment, and the academic gender gap. I label these five countries as liberal states, a term that is frequently used in policy comparisons rather than gender studies. I also contextualize the academic gender gap within broader issues of policy concerns such as university funding, labour regulation, and global market trends.

Why call these countries liberal states? Decades ago, Esping-Andersen (1990) distinguished between three worlds of welfare capitalism, contrasting liberal states to both the corporatist ones in Western Europe and their social democratic counterparts in Northern Europe. He argued that these three "ideal types" reflect differing philosophical orientations to the role of the state in public life and especially to social spending. Esping-Andersen demonstrated that the liberal states relied on relatively unregulated markets and individual wage earners to maintain productivity and well-being, and that social provision was largely targeted to the poor and needy. In contrast, the corporatist states focused more on maintaining the wages of middle-income earners, whereas social democratic states provided universal benefits and services to all citizens in an attempt to promote equality.

Esping-Andersen argued that countries in each cluster have always shared policy solutions, especially during the development of employment standards and welfare programs from the 1930s to the 1970s. Although aspects of his schema have been disputed, classifying countries into similar types remains useful for comparative research.[5] I argue that Australia, Canada, New Zealand, the United Kingdom, and the United States continue to share policy solutions relating to labour market and university restructuring. They also reveal similar trends in family and work, which are discussed in more detail in Chapter 2 (Baker 2001, 2010b; Kamerman and Kahn 1997; O'Connor, Orloff, and Shaver 1999; OECD 2007a, 2008b).

In the liberal states, patterns of educational attainment, employment trends, the rising percentage of female doctorates, and gendered aspects of university-based academic work have been shown to be similar (Auriol 2007; Brooks 1997; Currie, Thiele, and Harris 2002; Kingfisher 2001; OECD 2007a, 2009a). For example, about half of new PhDs in these countries are now earned by women, and women comprise nearly half of new full-time academic university appointments and about 20 percent of senior positions (Auriol 2007; CAUT 2011b; Lipsett 2008; Monroe et al. 2008). For these reasons, the book discusses the liberal states collectively, arguing that restructuring trends and the gender gap cross international borders.

Nevertheless, some differences must also be acknowledged. For example, Australia, Canada, and the United States are divided into states or provinces, which have developed their own educational systems, creating many internal variations. Some liberal states and the jurisdictions within them invest more public money than others in postsecondary education and research. Academic salaries also vary considerably by jurisdiction and by institution (CAUT 2011a, 55-57; Falks 2010). The United States has more private universities than the other liberal states, and its government contributes less public funding to the postsecondary sector (CAUT 2011a, 57). In addition, promotional systems and ranks vary, especially between North American universities and those in Australia, New Zealand, and the United Kingdom. Gendered patterns of employment after motherhood for all women and for academics differ slightly by jurisdiction: rates of maternal employment are higher in North America than in the other liberal states (OECD 2009c).

Within a jurisdiction, differences also exist between universities, relating to their public/private status, predominant forms of funding, strategic goals, size, national or international prestige, and the composition of their student body (Auriol 2007; Fisher et al. 2009; OECD 2009a). In official statistics, universities are often categorized into two broad types: the first is research/medical/doctoral, and the second is teaching/undergraduate/baccalaureate, because universities within these broad institutional types tend to share many of the same priorities and practices. Some official statistics, such as those in Canada, also use an intermediate category of "comprehensive" university (CAUT 2011a, 57).

Although this book refers to research and teaching universities, I also argue that the historical differences between the two types are becoming blurred as more institutions pressure their academics to increase their research productivity, obtain external research funding, and develop collaborative research networks that are sometimes international. This is particularly predominant in countries with national research assessment exercises, which include Australia, New Zealand, and the United Kingdom (discussed further in Chapter 3). Canada and the United States have not established national research assessment schemes, as the provinces and states have retained jurisdiction over education. However, I suggest that pressures to increase research productivity influence universities in all the liberal states and that many of the former teaching universities are becoming more comprehensive.

In the first two chapters, comparative statistics reveal similar patterns in paid and unpaid work throughout the liberal states, which I maintain are influenced by political and socioeconomic forces that tend to be international. In addition, I reveal that gender relations are altered in similar ways by these global changes in work.

What Is the Academic Gender Gap?

Volumes have been written about the academic profession, but this book focuses on the changing academic gender gap in a restructuring university environment. This concept refers to the varying qualifications and experiences of male and female scholars employed in universities, including differences in job security, institutional affiliation, working hours, rank, salary, job satisfaction, collegial networks, and length of career. Over the decades, the gender gap has diminished substantially if one measures it by indicators such as the rising percentage of female doctorates and faculty, as well as the gender differences in promotion and salary.

Significantly more women now receive PhDs and find permanent positions within universities than during the 1970s (Brooks 1997; Glazer-Raymo 2008; Long 2001; Sussman and Yssaad 2005). In Canada, for example, the percentage of female full-time university teachers increased from 13 in 1970 to 34 in 2008, and 45 percent of full-time university teachers newly appointed in 2007-08 were women (CAUT 2009, 2010, 18). Similar developments have occurred in the other liberal states (Auriol 2007; Carrington and Pratt 2003; Lipsett 2008; New Zealand Ministry of Education 2009), as shown in more detail in Chapter 2, though comparable statistics for each of the five countries are not always available for the same years.

Notable improvements in the rank of female academics are apparent in recent decades, but women are still disproportionately clustered in junior positions. In the universities of the liberal states, men occupy between 76 and 82 percent of senior positions, a drop from 90 to 95 percent in the 1960s (Carrington and Pratt 2003; CAUT 2011b; New Zealand Human Rights Commission 2008; Sussman and Yssaad 2005; AAUP 2006).[6] In all the liberal states, male academics are more likely to work full-time with fewer career interruptions, to publish more peer-reviewed articles, and to be promoted to higher ranks with higher salaries in a promotion system that often favours research over teaching and service (Brooks 1997; Brooks and Mackinnon 2001; Monroe et al. 2008; Nakhaie 2007).

As more women enter the academic profession at the lower ranks, there is clear evidence that intergenerational change has been occurring. The gender gap, however, cannot be attributed solely to age cohort or the fact that fewer women received doctorates in the past. Research suggests that gendered family circumstances, household responsibilities, and personal priorities help preserve the gap (Bassett 2005; Bracken, Allen, and Dean 2006; Comer and Stites-Doe 2006; Monroe et al. 2008; Settles et al. 2006). Differences have also been explained on the basis of institutional discrimination and marginalization in collegial networks, sometimes referred to as a "chilly climate" for academic women and an "unbreakable glass ceiling" (Curtis 2005; Drakich et al. 1991; Drakich and Stewart 2007; Valian 1998; Wagner, Acker, and Mayuzumi 2008).[7] Systems of hiring and promotion have also been cited as reasons for the perpetuation of the gender gap.

Academic Practices and University Restructuring

One problem with discussing academic priorities and practices across the liberal states is that differing terminology is often used for the same things. For example, academics are typically called faculty in North America but academic staff in the other countries. Education beyond secondary school is normally called postsecondary or higher education in North America but tertiary education in the other countries. Degrees beyond the undergraduate level are often called graduate degrees in North America and postgraduate in the other countries. Gaining job security in North America involves a rigorous process called tenure, but this is known as confirmation or permanence in the other countries and is sometimes less arduous. In this book I normally use the North American terminology, sometimes noting others in parentheses, but have also tried to find generic terms that are less confusing.

One reason for discussing the liberal states collectively is that university practices and priorities are often said to vary more by institutional type than by jurisdiction (Fletcher et al. 2007; Geiger 2004). As noted above, universities are often divided into two main types – research and teaching – although the intermediate category called comprehensive is used as well. Universities are also ranked both nationally and internationally, and the research universities typically receive higher ratings (discussed in Chapter 3). This book focuses on research and teaching universities to highlight the gender differences in job location and institutional prestige. Decades ago, Jessie Bernard (1964) discussed the sexual division of labour evident in American universities, where men more often concentrated on knowledge creation in the research universities, and women tended to specialize in teaching and the pastoral care of students, especially in the women's colleges.

Historically, research universities have placed considerable pressure on academics to create new knowledge, as well as teach, supervise research students, and contribute to decision making in the institution and profession (Caplow and McGee 1958; Jencks and Riesman 1977). Many research universities, especially in North America, continue to accentuate knowledge creation partly by using temporary (or sessional) lecturers to teach some of the larger undergraduate classes and paying them on a course-by-course basis or for one or more sessions or semesters. This strategy, which saves university salary money and frees up senior academics for graduate supervision and research, has been increasingly applied since the late 1970s. In fact, many universities in the liberal states are restructuring to strengthen their focus on research productivity, to gain more external funding, and to heighten their international reputation (Dobbie and Robinson 2008; Glazer-Raymo 2008; Lucas 2006; Mohrman, Ma, and Baker 2008). I argue that this trend, which is underpinned by economic pressures, tends to augment the academic gender gap.

The teaching universities have historically concentrated on classroom instruction and assisting undergraduate students to gain a general education, with fewer expectations that faculty will train future researchers or become producers of new knowledge themselves. In recent decades, some colleges, polytechnic institutes, and teacher training schools have been converted into teaching universities, or merged with existing universities, and continue to provide vocational training as well as undergraduate education. There is some evidence that teaching universities have hired and promoted more women academics than the research universities and have also introduced more classroom innovations (CAUT 2009; Fletcher et al. 2007; New Zealand Human Rights Commission 2008). However, they usually require scholars to spend more time on class contact hours, the pastoral care of students, and other teaching-related activities, even when they increase expectations of research productivity.

Academic practices vary somewhat by institutional governance and funding. Most universities in Australia, Canada, New Zealand, and the United Kingdom are publicly funded and therefore must abide by government regulations and guidelines. However, they can also be privately funded, as many are in the United States. Private universities differ from public ones in a number of ways, including lower rates of unionization, which could influence working conditions, job security, and salaries (Wickens 2008).

Terms of university hiring and promotion are usually specified in collective agreements between management and professional associations or labour unions, but the laws governing collective bargaining differ by jurisdiction. Unionization rates also vary substantially by jurisdiction but also by the public or private status of the university, by the individual university, by departments within them, and the employment status of academics (part-time/full-time or temporary/permanent). Current unionization rates are difficult to ascertain and compare cross-nationally, but Wickens (ibid.) notes that in the United States, less than 40 percent of full-time faculty members were unionized in 1995. Labour unions are more often found in the public universities, but unionization rates appear to be rising, including in private universities and among part-time or temporary workers, many of whom are graduate students (ibid.).

In Canada, where most colleges and universities are publicly funded, unionization rates appear to be higher than in the United States, but these rates vary considerably by informational source and how they are calculated. Rhoades (1998) states that 44 percent of full-time faculty in Canadian universities were represented by collective bargaining agents in the mid-1990s compared to 65 percent of employees in other public institutions. Dobbie and Robinson (2008) give a much higher figure, referring to union density of 79 percent in 2004, but without providing a reference. However, James Turk, executive director of the Canadian

Association of University Teachers (pers. comm., 30 August 2011), verified this 79 percent figure, which suggests a considerable increase in university unionization during the past decade. Although I contacted the Tertiary Education Union in New Zealand, it was unable to provide a unionization rate for full-time academics in that country.

Even when a trade union is present in a university, not all academics become union members.[8] In some countries, university managers have attempted to undermine unions by offering individual contracts to academics, as well as special arrangements for leave and supplemental benefits that fall outside the collective agreement.[9] Dobbie and Robinson (2008) note that greater unionization in Canada and the United States during recent years has stalled neither the decline in tenured faculty relative to part-timers nor the corporatization of higher education.

Hiring and Promotion

Before the 1970s, university-based academic work (as well as other professional employment) was often hierarchical and dominated by powerful managers and "old-boy ties" (Bernard 1964; Epstein 1971). In some universities, deans and department heads were permitted to make decisions about hiring and promotion with few written guidelines or consultations with other academics. The most prestigious universities hired from top graduate schools, accepted few women, expected their academics to generate research papers as well as teach students, and assumed that the most productive of them would use the global academic marketplace to their advantage (Caplow and McGee 1958). Less prominent universities were more likely to hire local graduates and women, as well as strong teachers with fewer publications. In recent decades, however, promotion rules have become more formalized, decisions are typically made by committees, and a number of equity initiatives have been introduced at the institutional and departmental level.

Universities normally hire academics in both temporary and permanent employment. The tenure-stream positions, which are expected to lead to permanent jobs, are the most often advertised, sometimes internationally, and hiring decisions are usually made by committees comprised of academics with oversight by academic managers. To qualify for these positions, candidates increasingly require a PhD as well as university teaching experience and scholarly publications or conference papers based on their research.[10] They must also fit in with the teaching, administrative, and research needs of the university and department, which are not always readily apparent to applicants.

Several years after their first tenure-stream appointment, academics are normally expected to apply for tenure or relative job security.[11] Many procedural variations exist, but universities typically require some form of written application based on evidence of sustained performance in teaching, service, and research. The rigour of this process varies considerably according to institutional prestige and jurisdiction, requiring proof that performance and productivity are anywhere from acceptable to exceptional.

Many universities also provide annual salary increases and/or cost-of-living adjustments within each rank without requiring a promotion application, as well as merit pay for exceptional performance shown in annual reviews. However, formal applications are obligatory for promotion into the next rank (such as from assistant professor to associate professor in North America, and from lecturer to senior lecturer in the other countries). In this process, universities typically expect candidates to submit extensive dossiers listing their accomplishments in teaching, service, and research, and also require them to provide written justifications for promotion. Although most institutional guidelines indicate that all three areas of teaching, service, and research are important for tenure and promotion, the larger and more prestigious universities tend to give more weight to research productivity, peer esteem, and international reputation, especially for promotion beyond the junior ranks (Brooks and Mackinnon 2001; Monroe et al. 2008; Nakhaie 2007; Ornstein, Stewart, and Drakich 2007; White 2004).

With globalizing labour markets, more academics are now seeking promotional jobs in other countries, as productive researchers are often able to improve their rank and status by acquiring external job offers and changing universities. Highly valued individuals can also use job offers from other universities to bargain for additional resources at their current workplace or threaten to leave for a better position elsewhere. Geographic mobility has always been viewed as an advantage to academic bargaining and promotion (Caplow and McGee 1958; Jencks and Riesman 1977). For example, Bernard (1964) argued that female scholars in the United States, especially married mothers, were typically less mobile than their male counterparts, which put them at a disadvantage in the academic marketplace. Negotiating for more resources with little intention of actually accepting a job offer is generally frowned upon by unions and academic colleagues, and is less likely to be effective in universities with strong unions and formalized rules about remuneration.

Work Expectations

As academics reach the middle and higher ranks, they are normally required to contribute to university decision making as well as professional activities such as peer reviewing articles, book manuscripts, and grant applications. They would also be expected to publish their research widely in scholarly journals and books, fund their research via internal and external grants, and develop national or international research networks. They might perform consulting work for governments or other organizations but are generally expected to raise their university's profile through their professional activities. Increasingly, universities are developing prestigious research chairs, which are top academic positions funded from private donations or new state resources. These chairs usually involve high salaries, reduced teaching loads, and considerable status, and they are much more likely to be held by men than by women (Reimer 2004; Side and Robbins 2007; Slaughter and Leslie 1999).

Increasingly, and particularly in the top research universities, academics who have not accrued sufficient publications, contributed significantly to their institution, or gained a national or international reputation will not be promoted to the highest rank before they reach the age of retirement. Historically, most scholars in Australia, New Zealand, and the United Kingdom never progressed to the rank of professor, because each department contained only one professor, who served as head of department for an indefinite period. Now that head of department is usually a fixed-term position lasting less than five years, there could be several professors in a department, and a lower-ranking individual could become its head or chair.[12]

Hiring and promotion have become more competitive in an international labour market with shrinking government contributions to operating costs. Academics must now focus even more on research productivity and entrepreneurial research activities to progress through the ranks. Mothers with young children have fewer opportunities to undertake such projects, but feminists also suggest that whatever tasks women perform in their employment are typically granted less recognition and remuneration than men's (Brooks 1997; Daly and Rake 2003).

Institutional Restructuring
In recent decades, universities have undergone significant institutional changes as their socioeconomic environments have been redefined. Numerous researchers have analyzed these changes, revealing similar trends in the liberal states.[13] In many jurisdictions, student enrolments and university operating costs have typically risen faster than government grants to public universities since the 1970s (Fisher et al. 2009; Sikes 2006). In Canada, government funding as a percentage of university operating revenue declined from 84 percent in 1978 to 58 percent in 2008, whereas tuition fees paid by students increased from 12 to 35 percent (CAUT 2011a, 2). In New Zealand, universities now receive only 45 percent of their annual income from government grants (NZVC 2010), down considerably from the 1970s.

To compensate for diminished state funding, many institutions have raised tuition fees and recruited more international or out-of-state students, often charging them higher fees than domestic or local students. They have also sought more external funding, especially from alumni and corporate donors. To increase "flexibility" and control labour costs, they have hired more temporary or part-time academics. In the United States, the percentage of faculty who were full-time and tenured declined from 36.5 in 1975 to 24.1 in 2003 as universities hired more part-timers and temporary faculty (West and Curtis 2006, 7).

Another significant change is that public universities now tend to operate more on a corporate model rather than a public service one, with stringent accountability measures, greater demands to diversify funding sources, and even expectations of profit making in some instances (Brenneis, Shore, and Wright 2005; Chan and Fisher 2008; Marginson and Considine 2000; Metcalfe 2010; Mohrman, Ma, and Baker 2008; Slaughter and Leslie 1999). The growth of accountability regimes means that university managers place a stronger emphasis on efficiency and effectiveness. Public universities have also increased their use of national and international benchmarking to compare their performance with similar institutions and to rank institutional and departmental productivity, status, and achievements (CAUT 2011a, 56; Taylor and Braddock 2007; Turk 2000).

The market for university faculty, staff, and students has also become increasingly international. More students receive their degrees outside their hometowns than they did in the 1970s. Graduate students from Australia, Canada, and New Zealand travel to other countries, such as the United States and the United Kingdom, to attain master's and doctoral degrees from prestigious institutions. Many academics also work in universities in other countries for a portion of their career. For example, 40.8 percent of university teachers currently working in Canada are either non-permanent residents or originally were immigrants (although most of these would now be Canadian citizens) (CAUT 2011a, 20).

In addition, scholars are expected to review and publish articles for international as well as national journals and to prepare and review book manuscripts for publishing companies located in other countries as well as their own. They also prepare reference letters or promotion assessments for colleagues and department heads in other countries. They receive visiting scholars and go abroad for conferences, research projects, and sabbatical leave. All these factors contribute to an international job market for academics and the convergence of academic standards and practices among the liberal states.

At the same time, universities have expanded their academic programs and taken advantage of new technologies and distance learning in order to teach or attract more students and increase their revenue. They have also accepted a more diverse range of students in terms of age, sex, parental status, social class, and race/ethnicity, which has required the creation of more student services as well as changes in teaching style. Public universities have been pressured by their governments, professional associations, and staff and student unions to develop equity initiatives and family-friendly guidelines to accommodate the growing diversity among students and academics. Many institutions have established student equity programs and campus day care centres, and have expanded employment-related programs such as parental leave, flexible working hours, and gender-based mentoring for scholars.

All these issues will be discussed in more detail in later chapters. However, the trends suggest that although universities have become more cognizant of equity and diversity, they have also grown more managerial and capitalist in their attempts to increase revenue and to compete nationally and internationally (Fisher et al. 2009; Metcalfe 2010; Slaughter and Leslie 1999; Turk 2000). This is apparent in the public universities of all the liberal states because they are influenced by similar market trends, neo-liberal initiatives, and patterns of demography, migration, and human rights, which encourage a convergence of institutional practices. However, stronger international and research pressures are more apparent in the research universities than in their teaching counterparts.

The Book's Theoretical Framework

This book draws on feminist political economy theories, social capital theory, and interpretive frameworks. First, feminist political economy theories suggest that people's lives are shaped by their access to social, institutional, and material resources that are unequally distributed between men and women (Bakker and Silvey 2008; Luxton 2006; Vosko 2002). Therefore, I have situated this study within the wider economic and political context of global market changes, which have encouraged many workplaces, including universities, to restructure. I argue that certain types of restructuring tend to augment the gender gap.

Since the 1970s, governments in the liberal states have been signing freer trade agreements with other countries while strengthening work incentives and weakening labour legislation. Greater emphasis on market forces has encouraged many employers to become more efficient and productive, to reduce their operating costs, increase their revenue sources, and expand into foreign markets. To accomplish these goals, they often create flexible and specialized labour forces, partly by hiring more temporary workers (Armstrong and Armstrong 2004; Banting and Beach 1995; Easton 2008; Fairbrother and Rainnie 2006; Kalleberg 2011). However, this reinforces a dual labour market, which consists of "good" jobs and "bad" jobs (Torjman and Battle 1999).

Typically more secure and better paid, the former are often protected by labour legislation and/or union contracts. The latter are accompanied by less security, fewer employment benefits, and lower wages. On average, good jobs are more likely to be gained by white, middle-class, educated employees with fewer family responsibilities, whereas bad jobs are more often done by students, visible minorities, less educated workers, and mothers with daily responsibilities for young children (Bakker and Silvey 2008; Easton 2008; Vosko 2000; Vosko, MacDonald, and Campbell 2009; Walby et al. 2007). These economic and political changes have altered practices in many workplaces, including universities. More details of university restructuring will be discussed in Chapter 3, but I show throughout this book that many of the part-time and temporary positions in universities are occupied by doctoral students, partnered women, and mothers. Academic men are more likely to find full-time permanent jobs at the more prestigious universities and to progress through the ranks of academia.

The book draws heavily on research and theories about the impact of domestic divisions of labour on paid work in the current competitive environment. I maintain that typical patterns of marriage, where women partner with older and professionally established men, tend to augment the social expectations that they will shoulder the domestic and care work, creating a "second shift" of after-hours household work, especially for employed mothers (Hochschild 1989, 1997; Johnson and Johnson 2008). More often than men, women accept the day-to-day responsibilities of childrearing and housework, which gives them less time and motivation than men to pursue full-time careers or to gain promotion (Bittman and Pixley 1997; England 2010; Grummell, Devine, and Lynch 2009; Kitterød and Pettersen 2006; McMahon 1999; Ranson 2009). When men and women become parents, they often make differing choices and negotiate space for different activities, based on their gender and social/ material resources (B. Fox 2009).

I particularly rely on the "motherhood penalty" research because it shows that the careers of mothers tend to lag behind those of childless women and fathers (Budig and England 2001; Correll, Benard, and Paik 2007; Crittenden 2001; Portanti and Whitworth 2009). This research suggests that employed mothers are typically viewed by employers and co-workers as less committed and ambitious than fathers or child-free women. The careers of mothers tend to progress at a slower pace because having and raising children sometimes requires them to take time off work or reduce their employment hours, especially if they live in families where care and household management are seen as women's work. They themselves sometimes choose to give priority to their children while they are preschoolers, hoping to return to full-time work at a later date. However, taking leave or reducing working hours is often consequential, especially for professional careers such as university teaching and research.

Second, the book draws on social capital theory. In the wider research, human and cultural capital usually refers to personal characteristics, skills, and qualifications that lead to employment, economic gain, or social mobility (Bourdieu 1977, 1986; Coleman 1988). The concept of social capital has been defined in various ways by different authors, but it generally refers to connections that can be used to gain access to social support, advice, information, protection, powerful positions, or economic gain, and that might contribute to feelings of belonging or community well-being (Bourdieu 1986; Putnam 2000). Bourdieu (1988) also differentiated between academic capital and intellectual capital, the former referring to integration and respect from colleagues in the university work environment.

For university-based scholars, attaining human and social capital would include earning a doctorate at a prominent university; developing research, writing, and collaborative skills; knowing how to get published and how to sell their research to other academics; acquiring the confidence to lecture and publish widely; and gaining the respect of colleagues. Throughout this book, the research suggests that for various reasons relating to upbringing, marriage patterns, care responsibilities, and access to professional support and resources, women are less likely than

men to attain the human and social capital necessary to compete equit-
ably in the university environment (Beck and Young 2005; Bourdieu
1977; van Emmerik 2006).

Third, the book draws on interpretive perspectives that acknowledge
the differing subjectivities and identities of equally qualified people working in the same occupation (Thomas and Davies 2002). Interpretive
 theories generally suggest that the meanings associated with particular
actions or behaviours are socially constructed. This indicates that our
subjectivities (including self-image, gender identity, attitudes, and decisions) are shaped by the ways in which we present ourselves to others
and how they interpret, ignore, resist, or reinforce our actions (Butler
1990; Goffman 1959). I particularly rely on performance theories of
gender, suggesting that masculinity and femininity are not what people
are but what they *do* (Kimmel 2008; West and Zimmerman 1987).

The interpretive approach acknowledges that academic women and
men sometimes develop differing priorities and make varying life choices,
which is aptly demonstrated by some of the participant quotes from my
research. However, even when the behaviour of academic women resembles that of academic men, it can be viewed, evaluated, and legitim-
ated differently (Glazer-Raymo 2008; Kelan 2009; Probert 2005). I suggest
that these differences are shaped by gendered social expectations but
also by access to social support and material resources.

Although I focus on sex differences and the social construction of
gender, I also acknowledge the relevance of intersectionality, a concept
suggesting that the impact of sex on employment status may be com-
pounded or alleviated by other factors, such as age, rank, marital status,
sexual preference, ethnicity, culture, race, and institutional setting.
Furthermore, I realize that not all women or men share the same ambitions, employment experiences, or domestic circumstances, even when
they gain the same qualifications or rank, work in the same profession
or institution, or share cultural backgrounds. Clearly, individuals differ.
Furthermore, people often modify their attitudes and ambitions over
time, with maturity but also with changes in their living arrangements,
parental status, and circumstances in the workplace. The impact of
gender could combine with any of these other factors to alter job status
or acceptance within collegial networks (Kobayashi 2002; Kosoko-Lasaki,

Sonnino, and Voytko 2006). This book focuses on male/female experiences and social interpretations of gender in university workplaces in the liberal states, while acknowledging some of these other factors, particularly age, rank, and type of university.

The Research Basis of the Book

Academic Careers and the Gender Gap is based on several types of research sources, including international and national statistics and reports; studies on work, academic priorities, and the academic gender gap; and my own interviews with academics in two eras and countries. The book also draws on my personal career experience, which spans thirty-eight years and includes postsecondary teaching and research work in four of the five liberal states. In the feminist and qualitative research tradition, this experience contributes insider knowledge to the analysis of the academic gender gap.

Contextual data are provided for all the liberal states by drawing on statistics from the Organisation for Economic Co-operation and Development (OECD), national statistics, and other comparative studies. More data are offered for Canada than for the other countries because the book is published there and because one of the empirical studies took place there. The other empirical study was done in New Zealand, but fewer comparable statistics are available from that country. In fact, finding comparable statistics for all the liberal states has been challenging. Some of the gaps are influenced by divergent definitions, an emphasis in official statistics on variables other than male/female differences, and inaccessible or costly data in some jurisdictions.

My Interview Studies

One study was carried out in Canada in 1973 and the other in New Zealand in 2008 (for further details, see the Appendix on page 175). Both were grounded in qualitative research, which is not intended to discover causes or correlations or to test hypotheses. Instead, it is designed to flesh out the details of people's lived experiences and to investigate their subjectivities. Comments from interview participants can often complement quantitative findings by heightening understanding of the reasons behind the statistical correlations.

Both studies focused on participants' perceptions of the impact of gender and marital and parental status on academic careers as well as their observations of the university and social context in which they worked. Both were based on face-to-face qualitative interviews in which subjects were encouraged to elaborate on their family and academic backgrounds, their partners and personal relationships, their mentors, and the priorities and practices of their universities. The 2008 interviews further noted the influence of institutional type (that is, research versus teaching university) on their work environment.

Throughout the book, I argue that, despite their distance from each other and their differences in size, Canada and New Zealand have experienced roughly comparable academic practices and gendered work. Whereas Canada's population is about 34 million (Statistics Canada 2011), New Zealand's is just over 4 million (Immigration New Zealand 2011). Although many academic practices are similar in the two countries, the rank and tenure system in Canada tends to follow the North American model, whereas New Zealand's is closer to that of Australia and the United Kingdom. Both Canada and New Zealand are bicultural countries, and they also share similar laws and social policies as well as socio-demographic trends (Baker 2001, 2006).[14] In particular, both have experienced similar increases in women's educational attainment and percentages of women in the senior ranks of academia, comparable academic hiring/promotion practices, and high rates of foreign-born scholars.

My first study, completed in 1973, was situated in a research university in western Canada and began with an analysis of the extent of the academic gender gap and factors contributing to it, as well as a discussion of academic practices in North American universities. The empirical portion consisted of interviews with thirty-nine women working in male-dominated departments of this large urban and public university at a time when women formed 13.5 percent of full-time tenure-stream or tenured faculty.[15] In 1973, nearly all the departments of this university had a majority of male academics, and some contained few or no women.

The period in which this study occurred coincided with the second phase of the feminist movement and several studies of women's status such as the Report of the Royal Commission on the Status of Women in Canada (1970) and university-based investigations.[16] In this particular university, the vast majority of faculty were white, with North American or European origins. The study participants were white women of European/North American backgrounds. I contacted them by telephone and invited them to participate in a face-to-face interview with me in their office; the interviews, which lasted about one hour, used a schedule that was partially open-ended. The sample consisted mainly of full-time academics, from assistant professor to full professor, but also included some temporary lecturers, doctoral students, and several former doctoral students who had recently withdrawn from the program. Interviewing this latter group was designed to uncover why they had left their doctoral studies.

Many of the scholars at this Canadian university had migrated from the United States to take up positions (or to accompany their academic husbands) during the expansion of postsecondary education in the 1960s and 1970s. This suggests that geographic mobility was important to the academic profession even then. The project focused on the inconsistencies between the university discourse of academic merit and the realities of particularism as encountered by these women. It also explored their subjective experiences of being female in a male-dominated profession, as well as their role models and mentors, their career trajectories, and their personal and family circumstances. However, it did not compare male and female academics, as I did in the 2008 study.[17] For more details, see the Appendix or Baker (1975).

The second study began with a survey of recent research on the academic gender gap and academic practices in the liberal states. The empirical portion included qualitative interviews completed in 2008 with thirty male and female academics working in two urban and public universities on the North Island of New Zealand. One was a large established research university that prided itself on its research and graduate education (as well as undergraduate teaching) and enjoyed a high national and international reputation. The second was also large but newer and more oriented to undergraduate teaching, with higher class contact hours for teaching staff, slightly higher percentage of women in senior positions, and a lower national and international profile.

The subjects in the 2008 study, most of whom were white with New Zealand/European backgrounds, were contacted by e-mail and invited to be interviewed by me or my graduate student assistant.[18] The thirty participants, all of whom had doctorates, worked in permanent academic positions in all ranks (lecturer, senior lecturer, associate professor, and professor) in the humanities and social sciences in the two universities. These academic units were selected because they contained a higher percentage of women than did departments such as science or engineering and because I wanted the departmental culture and working conditions to be relatively constant among the participants.[19]

Unlike the 1973 interviews, those of 2008 compared the views and experiences of both men and women, and they were digitally recorded and fully transcribed. I also compared the perceptions of the participants by type of university and by rank (sometimes grouping the lecturers and senior lecturers together as junior and intermediate positions, and the associate professors and professors together as senior positions, to show broader trends and maintain participant anonymity).

The interviews were not meant to form a systematic comparison of academics working in two jurisdictions and two different eras, as the study design and sampling of the projects differed slightly. Instead, the rich and subjective verbatim comments from both projects are used to enhance our understanding of findings from the wider research and to provide more insight into changes over time and across borders. The high level of detail about participants' circumstances is unavailable in official statistics or quantitative studies that focus mainly on correlations between variables. These details tend to humanize the research and deepen the analysis.

The Book's Contribution

This book contributes to social science and feminist research by analyzing the relations between globalizing workplaces and the formal/informal elements of their culture. It also examines the interconnections between personal/family circumstances, access to social and material support, career ambition, and perceptions of professional success. The book demonstrates that the socioeconomic and political environments of many universities have changed over the past forty years, pressuring academic managers to modify some of their institutional priorities and practices, with a number of gendered consequences. Nevertheless, many practices have remained relatively constant over the decades, and gender differences persist in the social/human capital of male and female scholars.

The chapters show that though the academic gender gap has diminished, it has persisted over the decades, cutting across national boundaries. Although it is most prevalent in the research universities, it remains widespread in universities throughout the liberal states. Through its use of colourful comments from the interviewees, the book illustrates the many differences as well as similarities in the careers, personal lives, and subjectivities of academics. Although we cannot generalize from these interviews alone, the book is underpinned by an extensive survey of the available research about the gender gap in the liberal states.

This volume acknowledges that public universities have made substantial improvements toward gender equity since the 1970s but argues that they have also responded to neo-liberal pressures by expecting academics to strengthen their focus on research productivity, funded research, and other entrepreneurial activities. These newer priorities contribute to gender inequities, but I also maintain that the academic gender gap is perpetuated by collegial interactions and gendered personal lives. This conclusion provides more serious challenges for institutional change.

Gendered Patterns of Education, Work, and Family Life   **2**

[My parents] thought that after I got my PhD I would settle down and be 'normal.' They felt that it was just something that I had to get out of my system. They brag about what I have done, but they think I'm deviant.

– PART-TIME LECTURER, CANADA, 1973

When you look at the glass ceiling and look at how many women are up there in the key decision making roles ... I know that gender counts.

– FEMALE LECTURER, NEW ZEALAND, 2008

How have the patterns of postsecondary education, work, and family life changed for men and women since the 1970s, and how have these patterns influenced academic careers? This chapter provides the necessary context for an analysis of the academic gender gap by examining trends in education and paid/unpaid work, ending with a focus on academic work in universities. It shows that in recent decades, educational attainment has increased for the general population but especially for women and that nearly half of recent doctorates in the liberal states are now granted to women. More women also enter and remain in the labour force after motherhood. Women's earnings have become more important to households as living costs increase, more couples separate, and the job market becomes more competitive. More women have also gained university faculty positions, but a gender gap remains, especially at the higher ranks.

This chapter begins the argument, continued throughout the book, that many of the factors contributing to the academic gender gap are actually more generic issues relating to gendered patterns of work and family life. Like other women, female doctorate holders are still more likely than their male counterparts to specialize in disciplines leading to lower paying jobs, to work part-time, to occupy positions of less prestige, and to have shorter careers. I show in this chapter that childbearing and the "motherhood penalty" are clearly consequential for female employees, including women with doctorates and academic jobs. The chapter begins with an overview of socio-demographic and policy changes that have influenced women's educational attainment and employment patterns over the past four decades.

Socio-Demographic and Policy Changes

Since the 1970s, a number of socio-demographic trends and policy reforms have enabled women to prolong their education and to seek paid employment. These social changes have both epitomized and reinforced women's economic need and personal desire to break out of traditional domestic roles. For example, legal marriage rates have declined, whereas cohabitation rates and the average age of marriage have increased (Baker 2010b). Fertility rates have diminished considerably since the 1960s with improvements in contraception, higher costs of raising children, and less need for children to contribute to household subsistence or to support their parents in old age.

Despite high social expectations of childbearing, about 15 to 20 percent of women in the liberal states do not reproduce (ibid.). Childlessness tends to be associated with women's high educational attainment, high earnings, and stable employment, but for men it is associated with low education and earnings (Hagestad and Call 2007; Portanti and Whitworth 2009). Having fewer or no children for both sexes is also correlated with leaving the parental home and gaining postsecondary education later in life and marrying at an older age (ibid.). Most academic men delay having children until they complete their doctorates and find permanent work, but academic women with doctorates and full-time jobs are less likely than their male counterparts to marry or to become parents (Brooks 1997; Bassett 2005). This may involve a self-selection factor, but it could also indicate that academic success requires years of intensive work during women's childbearing years. It also suggests that marriage and childrearing represent differing expectations and work-loads for women and men.

In the early 1970s, when I undertook my Canadian academic study, legal marriage rates had reached the highest peak of the twentieth cen-tury, the age of marriage was relatively low, and attitudes toward un-married women were generally unfavourable (Baker 2010b; Beaujot 2000; Bittman and Pixley 1997). Few unmarried couples cohabited openly, and both men and women were pressured to marry and reproduce. Family laws in the liberal states designated the husband as the head of the household, and his place of residence was also the legal domicile of his wife and children. This made it difficult for wives to relocate to another city or jurisdiction to find work if their husband opposed it. If they moved without their husband's consent, the courts could view this as an act of marital separation, which became grounds for divorce. Furthermore, wives might be required to forfeit their right to spousal financial support and/or relinquish custody of their children (Backhouse 1991; Baker 2010b).

Now both males and females are encouraged to graduate from college or university and to secure paid work, but most adults still expect to find an intimate partner and enjoy a fulfilling family life. Furthermore, most people eventually marry even if they begin their conjugal life with cohabitation (Ambert 2005; Qu and Weston 2008), but social research indicates that some of the previous gendered expectations of marriage continue to linger. For example, Gerson (2009) found that young men in the United States still view themselves as the primary breadwinner in their future family and expect to have a "neotraditional" relationship with their female partner, who works for pay but looks feminine and provides home support. In contrast, young women are more likely than young men to expect an egalitarian relationship with shared domestic work in their family future, as well as satisfying paid work. In reality, more partnered men end up with full-time jobs, working longer hours and earning higher incomes than partnered women, who tend to become the main care providers even when they are employed full-time (Edlund 2007; Gerson 2009; Johnson and Johnson 2008; Ranson 2009).

In terms of social policy, human rights conventions and national laws have reinforced the rights of females to an equal education, employment equity, and fair remuneration. Employers and governments have been pressured by various interests, including trade unions, professional associations, women's groups, and international organizations such as the United Nations to change policies and practices to accommodate more women and mothers in the workforce (OECD 2007a). Most liberal states have introduced or expanded paid maternity/parental leave provisions, which have enabled pregnant women and new parents to retain their jobs and to gain seniority (Baker 2011a; Hantrais 2004).

Employers, governments, and unions have created employment equity initiatives for hiring and promotion, and developed or encouraged workplace childcare services (Baker 2011b; Brennan 2007; Jenson and Sineau 2001). They have also provided work-life balance programs designed to help employees reduce conflicts, largely by introducing more flexible hours and family-related leave for illness, emergencies, and bereavement. Several studies suggest that these kinds of programs have made little difference to the employment lives of most men (Bracken, Allen, and Dean 2006; Mason and Goulden 2004; OECD 2007a). However, they have undoubtedly helped many women retain their jobs, win promotion, and view themselves as paid workers as well as mothers and wives.

Family laws and social programs have become more gender-neutral, making less distinction between the legal obligations and responsibilities of husbands and wives, and of mothers and fathers (Baker 2006; Kamerman and Kahn 1997). At the same time, marriages have also become less stable, with more people moving in and out of marriage-like relationships (Beaujot 2000; Gray, Qu, and Weston 2007; Wu 2000). Until the early 1970s, the grounds for divorce were quite restrictive in most liberal states, but separation and divorce are now easier, less expensive, and more prevalent (Wu and Schimmele 2009).

Despite these changes, separated men tend to re-partner faster than their former wives and often create new households with younger women while their children continue to live most of the time with their mother. Fathers pay child support more often than in the past, with strengthened enforcement procedures in all the liberal states, but few men are required to pay spousal support or alimony (Baker 2010b). Consequently, more women need paid jobs to support themselves and their children outside marriage. Although labour markets have become more open for female workers, they have also become more competitive, and single mothers continue to struggle to make ends meet (Baker 2010d; Baker and Tippin 2002; Edin and Lein 1997; Walter 2002).

Postsecondary Educational Attainment and Gender

Since the 1970s, educational attainment among the general population has increased considerably, and university student enrolments have risen dramatically in all the liberal states. The gender balance of university students has also changed substantially, and first-time graduates are now more likely to be female (OECD 2009a, 21). For example, full-time university enrolment increased by 37 percent from 1998 to 2008 in Canada, and females comprised 58 percent of undergraduate students, 55 percent of master's students, and 47 percent of doctoral students in 2007-08 (CAUT 2010, 21). In 1966, only 8.0 percent of new PhDs in Canada were earned by women (Baker 1975, 86), but this had risen to 44.2 percent by 2008 (CAUT 2011a, 39).

The percentage of recent doctoral degrees earned by women is rapidly increasing in all the liberal states (Auriol 2007). Slightly over 50 percent of PhDs in the United States are now awarded to women (Council of Graduate Schools 2010), and close to 50 percent in Australia and New Zealand (Australian Government 2009; New Zealand Ministry of Education 2009). Table 2.1 shows the sex distribution of doctoral graduates in four of the five liberal states. Data from the United Kingdom are not available in a comparable format, except for individual universities,

Table 2.1 Recent doctoral graduates by sex and country, percentages of men and women

Country	Men	Women
Australia (2007)	51.5	48.5
Canada (2008)	55.4	44.2
New Zealand (2008)	50.3	49.7
United Kingdom (2008)	–	–
United States (2008-09)	49.6	50.4

Sources: Derived from Australian Government (2009, Table 2.1); CAUT (2011a, 39); New Zealand Ministry of Education (2009); United Kingdom National Statistics (2008); Council of Graduate Schools (2010, Table 2.25, 47).

whose pattern resembles that detailed in Table 2.1 (United Kingdom National Statistics 2008). In this table, the United States and New Zealand have the highest percentage of female doctorates.

When men and women enrol in doctoral programs, they tend to specialize in different areas. Most women are clustered in the health professions, education, fine arts, humanities, and social sciences, whereas men are far more numerous in engineering, applied sciences, mathematics, and the physical sciences, but even the male-dominated fields have had a much higher percentage of women in recent years (Auriol 2007; CAUT 2008a, 3). Disciplinary culture, doctoral requirements, and the nature of students also vary by specialization. For example, the median age at graduation differs by country, gender, and discipline. However, both men and women in education, the humanities, and social sciences take slightly longer to complete a PhD than in the natural sciences, engineering, or medical and agricultural science, where more financial support is available for doctoral students (Auriol 2010, 6; CAUT 2011a, 38).

Even when the area of specialization is controlled, women doctorates on average take a few months longer than men to finish their degrees (Auriol 2007, 11). In some cases, they could be taking maternity or family-related leave, but they could also be entering graduate studies at an older age or receiving less financial or other forms of support.

Table 2.2   Labour force participation rates of men and women with tertiary education, 2007

Country	Men	Women
Australia	93.0	81.3
Canada	90.0	83.0
New Zealand	93.2	79.9
United Kingdom	92.0	87.7
United States	91.1	79.8
OECD average	89.4	79.5

Source: Extracted from OECD (2009b, 258-66).

Although unemployment rates are usually lower for PhDs than for those with less education, women doctorates still have higher unemployment rates than men (ibid.).

Postsecondary Education and Gendered Employment Patterns

Since the 1970s, employment rates for women have increased as they gained higher educational qualifications (OECD 2009a, 73). Graduates of both sexes who invest long years of hard work to acquire a post-secondary or tertiary degree are more likely than those with less education to be motivated to use their degrees to find paid work. Nevertheless, male graduates are more likely than female graduates to participate in the labour force, as shown in Table 2.2 for the liberal states. Some minor cross-national variations are apparent in the gender employment gap, with a 7 percent difference between men and women in Canada and a 13 percent difference in New Zealand, but the patterns are similar in all these countries.

Among doctorate holders in the liberal states, men are more likely than women to be employed and to work full-time, as is shown in Table 2.3, though only for Australia and the United States. This table also indicates that both male and female PhDs have a much higher incidence of part-time work in Australia than in the United States. In explaining this, we need to be aware that Australia's definition of part-time work differs from that of the other liberal states (thirty-five hours or less instead

Table 2.3   Doctorates by full-time/part-time work and sex

Country	Full-time employment		Part-time employment	
	Male	*Female*	*Male*	*Female*
Australia (2001)	85.7	71.7	14.3	28.3
United States (2003)	94.8	86.5	5.2	13.5

Source: Auriol (2007, 16).

of thirty) and that it has a stronger culture of part-time maternal employment (OECD 2009c) as well as inducements for university-based academics to retire gradually through part-time work (Auriol 2007). In the United States, female doctorates have lower rates of part-time work than in Australia but are nearly three times more likely than men to work part-time. The availability of full-time jobs influences these trends as well, but part-time positions are typically used by mothers to help integrate earning and caring.

The National Graduates Survey in Canada (Statistics Canada 2009, Table A.3), based on the graduating class of 2005, indicated that 87 percent of male doctorates and 80 percent of female doctorates were working full-time two years after graduation. Another 4 percent of males and 10 percent of females were employed part-time, whereas 2 percent of men and 5 percent of women were outside the labour market. For women, the incidence of part-time work and leaving the job market would probably increase five to ten years later, as more become mothers and produce additional children. Also, the employment consequences of working part-time vary by age and stage in their career. Part-time work enables recent PhDs to gain experience, develop or maintain their professional interests, and earn some household money. However, these jobs seldom offer promotional opportunities or living wages.

Employment patterns also vary by area of educational specialization. For example, two years after graduation, Canadian doctorates in the humanities had the lowest rates of full-time employment, which may reflect the nature of the job market but also the large number of women in the humanities (Statistics Canada 2009, Chart 2.5). The highest rates of full-time employment are for doctorates in mathematics and computer and information sciences, reflecting the Canadian job market but also the high proportion of men in these fields. In addition, the earnings of doctoral graduates vary substantially by discipline, with the highest for business, management, and public administration (ibid., Chart 2.7.4). The average salary of women PhDs relative to men's also differs by subject area, with the smallest salary gap in education and fine arts (ibid.), where women's numbers are higher.

Cross-national comparisons indicate that about 76.0 percent of doctorate holders in Canada and 72.5 percent in the United States are "active in research," and many work in private industry or research centres. Only a third are classified as "teaching professionals" (Auriol 2007, 17), which suggests that most doctorates in these countries do *not* teach in colleges or universities. It is difficult to determine from existing studies whether or not PhDs who find academic work differ from those who accept other forms of employment, but there could be variations in career interests, family circumstances, and social capital.

Auriol (2010, 17) provides data from 1973 to 2006 for the United States, showing that the percentage of recent doctorates in science and engineering receiving full-time faculty positions diminished significantly throughout those years and that more accepted post-doctoral fellowships and other full-time positions. She also argues that although international exchange has always been an integral part of research work, it has increased with the globalization of the economy. Doctorate holders are a highly mobile population, and mobility is especially prominent among younger and more recent graduates (ibid.). Unfortunately, her report does not differentiate between men and women who leave the USA to study and work in other countries.

Education, Gender, and Parenting

More women now continue their studies to the highest levels of tertiary education, yet research suggests that high educational attainment tends to play out differently in the lives of men and women. First, the three tables above clearly indicate that men are most likely to use their qualifications to gain full-time employment and better earnings. Second, studies find that educated men are more likely than their female counterparts to marry and become fathers, and are less likely to separate, divorce, and become single parents (Baker 2010b; Ferber and Loeb 1997; M. Fox 2005; Hewlett and Vite León 2002; Jacobs 2004; Weedon et al. 2006). Third, educated men are more likely than comparable women to experience uninterrupted careers regardless of their parental or family circumstances. Even among highly educated professionals, the acceptance of family responsibilities appears to be unevenly distributed between men and women (Mason and Goulden 2002; O'Laughlin and Bischoff 2005).

Before the 1970s, few mothers with young children retained full-time professional careers, but more women in the liberal states now combine work and family. Paid maternity/parental leave is more readily available, and public childcare services are better developed and more affordable in all these countries (Baker 2011a, 2011b). However, labour markets have also become more competitive, making it difficult for workers to take long-term childrearing leave without financial or employment repercussions. If mothers quit their jobs, they may be unable to find comparable work when they are ready to re-enter the labour force. Should they take an extended parental leave, if that is permitted in their jurisdiction, they could find themselves temporarily disadvantaged in terms of household income. When they return to paid work, their extended leave could alter their subsequent duties and chances for promotion.

Australian research has found that women with university education tend to work longer hours for pay than other women but also that both men and women with university degrees spend more time with their children than do less educated people (Craig 2006). In all the liberal states, mothers are more likely than fathers to reduce their hours of paid work and increase their hours of unpaid labour after childbirth. In contrast, married or partnered fathers tend to take their earning obligations even more seriously by working full-time or overtime (OECD 2007a). Studies from many countries indicate that who cares for children and does the housework often coincides with conventional ideas about "performing gender" (Butler 1990; Kelan 2009), as well as interpersonal negotiations and the availability of household resources.

Table 2.4 Maternal employment rates, women 15-64 by country and age of youngest child, 2005

Country	0-16 years	Under 2 years	3-5 years	6-16 years	2 children under 15	3 children under 15
Australia	63.1	48.3	–	70.5	58.1	–
Canada	70.5	58.7	68.1	71.1	73.2	66.3
New Zealand	64.6	45.1	60.6	75.3	64.5	56.7
United Kingdom	61.7	52.6	58.3	67.7	62.4	42.3
United States	66.7	54.2	62.8	73.2	–	–
OECD	61.5	51.9	61.3	66.3	57.0	44.0

Source: Extracted from OECD (2007a, Table 3.2).

In both moderate-income and lower-income families, women continue to do much of the routine and daily indoor household tasks and caring work, whereas men do more of the occasional outside work, including maintenance and repairs for the house and the car (Baxter, Hewitt, and Haynes 2008; Johnson and Johnson 2008; Lindsay 2008; Ranson 2009). In higher-income families, couples often hire outsiders to do some house-work and most repairs; they may also send their young children to high-quality preschools or engage nannies or housekeepers to live in their home. However, these couples tend to retain a gendered division of labour for other household chores (Baker 2010b; Craig 2006).

The time and energy spent on domestic duties can certainly reduce incentives to spend long hours on paid work or to accept additional employment responsibilities that could lead to promotion, higher earnings, or greater peer esteem. Therefore, differences in family circumstances could have significant career outcomes for fathers and mothers. Table 2.4 shows that the liberal states share many similarities in maternal employment rates and that these rates vary by the age and number of children. However, the rates also fluctuate somewhat by country. The Australian figures are not divided in the same way as the others, but the table nevertheless indicates that the more children women have and the younger the children, the lower their employment rates, especially in Australia, New Zealand, and the United Kingdom. This table also

Table 2.5   Percentage of persons aged 25-54 working part-time by sex, presence of children, and country, 2000

Country	Women, no children	Mothers, 2 or more children	Men, no children	Fathers
Australia	40.8	63.1	8.0	6.9
Canada	17.0	30.7	5.2	4.3
New Zealand	20.6	50.8	5.9	5.6
United Kingdom	23.7	62.8	4.1	3.2
United States	10.1	23.6	3.5	1.8
OECD average	18.7	36.6	4.2	3.6

Source: OECD (2002, 78).

reveals that among mothers with preschool children, those in Canada are most likely to work for pay, suggesting more financial necessity, greater social approval of maternal employment, and/or better public support for maternity leave and childcare (Baker 2009c).

Single mothers report problems combining childrearing with paid work (Baker and Tippin 2002; Walter 2002). General employment rates for single parents (who are usually mothers) have increased over the past two decades, but they remain lower than for partnered mothers in the liberal states (OECD 2007a, 2008a). They also vary somewhat by jurisdiction: they are higher in North America than in Australia and New Zealand (ibid.). This suggests that employment rates for single parents are influenced by income support programs, childcare services, work incentives, wages, employment practices, and cultural values, as well as personal choices (in the UK, Australia, and New Zealand, single parents are referred to as "sole parents").

Table 2.4 (above) does not include information for men, but this is available in older figures from the OECD. The statistics in Table 2.5 are somewhat dated but nevertheless show that women's part-time employment rates are much higher than men's in all the liberal states. They are particularly high after motherhood and higher still for women who have two or more children. Retaining the responsibility for childcare clearly curtails female employment in all these countries. Regardless of education and occupation, employment differences are notable between mothers and non-mothers, and between men and women, although gendered employment rates are converging slightly in these countries.

Gendered Earnings and the Motherhood Penalty

In explaining gendered contributions to household income, researchers often refer to four factors: marriage patterns, gender discrimination in the labour market, the nature of women's jobs, and the priority mothers often give to family, which interferes with employability and career advancement. This book touches on all these issues but focuses especially on the relationship between perceptions of family responsibilities and patterns of paid work. Using the word "perceptions" does not imply that women and mothers do not *need* to care for children or frail parents but rather that their feelings of obligation, their style of care, and their standards of household work often differ from those of men and fathers.

When young men and women complete their education and begin their first job, their incomes are relatively similar (Beaujot 2000), although men often aim for more lucrative types of work. However, the gender wage gap tends to be augmented by the marriage gradient (Baker 2010b; Bernard 1982; Sue Wilson 2009). This refers to the statistical trend of women partnering with slightly older men who are already more established in their occupational lives, especially when couples re-partner in second and third relationships. The marriage gradient enables older husbands to assume (or to argue successfully) that they are the primary household earners whose work requirements should take priority if any conflict arises with family responsibilities. Granting precedence to the man's career also makes financial sense if he earns more household money than his wife. Both men and women typically perceive a good father to be a steady or high earner who faithfully supports his family (Connell 2000; Doucet 2006; Kelan 2009).

After partnering, women are more likely than men to make work-related concessions for their partner's career, including relocating when he finds an initial job or a promotion (Bassett 2005; Baker 2010d; McMahon 1999). Mothers are more likely than fathers to make work concessions for their children, including taking longer employment leave at childbirth, reducing their weekly working hours to care for their infants and young children, delaying application for promotion because they lack the confidence or energy to apply, or seeking a lower-paid job closer to home to enable the integration of earning, after-school child-care, and domestic chores (Baxter, Hewitt, and Haynes 2008; Probert 2005; Ranson 2009).

Sociological research has also suggested that parenting has become more intensive in recent decades, especially among the educated middle classes (Hays 1996; Wall 2009). Children are less often allowed to play outside unattended by adults and more often kept at home or driven long distances to various organized lessons and activities. This magnification of parenting, which is influenced by perceptions of "stranger danger" and the heightened importance granted to early learning for future success, has altered the lives of both mothers and fathers. However, the former are particularly involved in supervising and monitoring their children's daily activities. Generally, the more time and energy that parents spend on childcare and domestic activities, the less they have left for paid work.

Researchers have used the concept of the motherhood penalty, or child penalty, to refer to the employment consequences of childbearing and childrearing for women's earnings and promotional opportunities (Crittenden 2001; Zhang 2009). One indicator of the motherhood penalty is that potential job applicants or employees who are pregnant or mothers are perceived as less qualified, competent, and committed to the job than childless women or men, both in experimental situations and by real employers (Baker 2010d; Correll, Benard, and Paik 2007). Another indicator is that the statistical earnings gap between mothers and childless women is substantial. This gap tends to increase with women's age, their educational qualifications, job experience, the number of children they have, and the time they spend outside the labour force on caring activities (Budig and England 2001; Crittenden 2001; Zhang 2009).

In fact, the motherhood earnings gap can be higher than the gender wage gap for certain categories of mothers. For example, in Canada, forty-year-old childless women make about 30 percent more than comparable-aged mothers with three or more years of work interruption, whereas the earnings gap between Canadian men and women is 21 percent (Zhang 2009). Many mothers work part-time while their children are young, especially if they have a second or third child. In contrast, fathers with large families are more likely than any other category of employee to work full-time and overtime, and few fathers living with their children choose to work part-time (OECD 2007b, 57).

Despite the fact that child custody after marriage breakdown is legally based on the best interests of the child, few cases actually go to court and most children continue living with their mothers, as they did in the 1970s (Boyd 2003; Qu and Weston 2008; Wu and Schimmele 2009). More separated men than women re-partner, men re-partner faster, and they are more likely to choose younger spouses in their remarriages (Baker 2010b). This means that many mothers who were previously partnered live for at least part of their lives as single parents, limiting their time and energy for paid work. This is particularly relevant for mothers working in high-level professional jobs that require sustained career planning, intermittent travel, and entrepreneurial activities. Full-time tenured academic work has all of these characteristics.

Gender Differences in Academic Work

In all the liberal states, male doctorates are more likely than female doctorates to find full-time university jobs, especially in the higher-status research universities (Brooks 1997; CAUT 2008a; Nakhaie 2007; Probert 2005). For instance, women form 45.1 percent of tenure-track academic staff (who have not yet achieved job security) in Canadian teaching universities compared to only 38.5 in the research universities. Among tenured academics, they form 32.1 percent in teaching universities and only 26.8 percent in research universities (CAUT 2008b, 3). Statistics from 2004 also indicate that 21.5 percent of female faculty were full professors in Canadian teaching institutions compared to 17.2 percent in research institutions (CAUT 2008a, 5). In addition, the research universities tend to be granted higher status, as we will see in Chapter 3. Women full-time university teachers in Canada also tend to be younger than men, with fewer over fifty-five years of age (CAUT 2010, 13).

Second, female academics are more likely than their male equivalents to work part-time in all the liberal states. For example, in 2006-07, 41.8 percent of women academics working in United Kingdom universities did so part-time compared to 26.8 percent of men (Lipsett 2008). For early-career academics, part-time work seldom leads to promotion but focuses instead on enabling junior academics to gain teaching or research experience. Temporary teaching appointments also tend to offer fewer opportunities for research, publishing, and advancement through the ranks (Bellas and Toutkoushian 2003; Brooks 1997; Monroe et al. 2008). Although some academics use part-time work as a transition to retirement, this would not have the same negative career consequences as working part-time in early career.

Third, male academics report more satisfaction with their early-career mentoring, their job security, teaching loads, and advancement opportunities (Aisenberg and Harrington 1988; Bellas 1994; Curtis 2005; Drakich and Stewart 2007; Grummell, Devine, and Lynch 2009; Probert 2005; Sagaria 2007; Sax 2008; Toutkoushian, Bellas, and Moore 2007; Valian 1998; White 2004). Female academics also show higher attrition rates than their male counterparts and report higher levels of isolation, stress, and fatigue, as well as feelings of marginalization and under-utilization (Berberet et al. 2005; Carr et al. 2000). A number of studies suggest that in high-level professional jobs in general, more women than men tend to struggle for workplace recognition and collegial acceptance (Bacchi 1993; Gill et al. 2008).

Fourth, academic men working in universities have more peer-reviewed publications than women do in a promotional system that tends to value research over teaching (Burris 2004; Nakhaie 2002, 2007). However, publication rates are influenced by the type of jobs female faculty have. Women are disproportionally located in teaching institutions and departments with higher teaching loads and greater expectations of allocating time to the pastoral care of students. More women also work part-time, often in teaching positions with fewer expectations of knowledge creation. Their lower publication rates also relate to their areas of specialization, as the research culture, funding possibilities, and publication rates tend to be lower in the humanities, education, and social sciences, where most women faculty are located, than in the sciences and engineering, where men tend to cluster (Monroe et al. 2008; Ornstein and Drakich 2007).

Fifth, academic salaries continue to vary by gender, although the discrepancy is narrowing. In Canada, for example, the average salary of women full-time university teachers was 89.3 percent of men's in 2007, up from 85.5 percent in 2000 (CAUT 2009, 6; 2011b, 8). Canadian salaries are higher at the medical/doctoral universities than at the teaching/undergraduate universities, where more women work (CAUT 2011b, 7). However, salaries typically vary by jurisdiction, type of university, and academic discipline. Women's earnings relative to men's are the highest in fields with larger numbers of women, such as applied and fine arts, education, and the humanities (ibid., 8). Female full professors (who represent about 21 percent of all full professors in Canada) earned about 94 percent of men's salaries in 2008, which is above average for all university teachers in Canada (ibid.). All these statistics suggest that women's lower salaries are associated with disciplinary choices, the location of their academic jobs, their younger ages, and their predominance in the lower ranks. If we control for institutional type, age, and rank, the gender gap in salaries is smaller. Furthermore, women's salaries relative to men's have increased over the years.

As a general rule, the percentage of female academics tends to decrease as rank and job security increase, especially in the more prestigious research or medical/doctoral institutions. This is well illustrated by 2008 Canadian figures for full-time faculty: women constituted about 53 percent of lecturers, 44 percent of assistant professors, 36 percent of associate professors, and 21 percent of full professors (CAUT 2010, 16). Among full-time staff, more tenure-track than tenured positions are held by women: 43.1 percent compared to 30.2 percent (ibid., 17). Because so many "new hires" are female, the percentage of tenured women will probably increase in the future. However, we must also acknowledge that Canadian unemployment rates are higher for women than for male academics, especially for academics with children under six years (ibid., 18).

Comparable statistics from all the liberal states are not easily found, but a similar gendered hierarchy exists in these countries. Recent figures from the University of Auckland (New Zealand's largest university) indicate that women make up about 53 percent of lecturers, 47 percent of senior lecturers, 28 percent of associate professors, and 20 percent of professors (University of Auckland 2010, 43). Monroe et al. (2008) noted that 38 percent of full-time faculty in the United States are female, but only slightly more than 15 percent of them work in the top universities. To express this gender gap in other terms, they show that in the United States men comprise 85 percent of full professors, 80 percent of tenured faculty, and 65 percent of tenure-track faculty. The patterns are similar in the other liberal states (AAUP 2006; Bellas 1994; Brooks 1997; Falks 2010; White 2004).

Monroe et al. (2008) argue that female academics in the United States fare no better in terms of gender equity than do women in the general labour force. They are underrepresented in almost all disciplines and are less likely than men to hold tenure-track positions, be granted tenure, achieve full professorships, and receive equivalent salaries (ibid.). Studies show that many of these gendered patterns of work cut across professional and jurisdictional boundaries.

Conclusion

This chapter has revealed similar trends of education and gendered work in all the liberal states, with some minor cross-national variations in the details. Generally, more women than men are completing university degrees and almost half of recent doctoral graduates are now women. More women are working for pay, most of them in full-time positions, and many are progressing through the ranks of their chosen occupations (OECD 2007a). However, a gender gap remains in hours of paid work, types of jobs, and employment earnings, which is apparent in the general labour force as well as for PhDs and university-based academics. Indeed, many of the factors contributing to the academic gender gap are actually more generic issues relating to gendered patterns of work and family life. This gap is more apparent for mothers than for childless women and is particularly notable for single mothers.

Furthermore, women tend to assume more responsibility than men for unpaid domestic labour and for caregiving, and they make more work-related concessions for their partners, children, and other family members. These patterns have led researchers to compare the employment conditions and earnings of childless women and mothers, finding that, in terms of their rank and salaries, mothers tend to be penalized in the labour market for having and raising children. This motherhood penalty cuts across educational, occupational, and national boundaries. In fact, women with high levels of education and more senior professional or managerial jobs tend to face even more severe drawbacks than other women because they cannot take extended leave without negative employment consequences.

The next chapter focuses on university-based work and contains a fuller discussion of recent patterns of restructuring within the public universities of the liberal states. It argues that though institutional priorities have gradually changed, many academic expectations and practices have remained relatively constant. The basis for academic promotion at the top universities remains roughly the same as in the 1970s, with a continuing emphasis on peer-reviewed publications, funded research, and international scholarly reputation. However, the new research assessment exercises, international ranking systems, and greater competition for doctoral students and research "stars" have strengthened this focus even further, with gendered consequences.

University Restructuring and Global Markets

3

Universities have to become profit orientated ... Part of academia and part of being intellectual is having the time to think about things, to debate things ... That's being slowly being taken away by wanting measurable outputs, making money, and profit-driven types of things.

– FEMALE LECTURER, TEACHING UNIVERSITY, 2008

I've become more and more unhappy with the way that this university seems to be managed these days ... The creeping managerial style or the way in which human resources seem to be more and more dictating what we are and are not able to do.

– MALE SENIOR LECTURER, RESEARCH UNIVERSITY, 2008

To enhance our understanding of the current academic environment, this chapter provides additional details about the socioeconomic and political context of university workplaces and recent restructuring. The chapter acknowledges that university employment conditions have always varied somewhat by institutional type, jurisdictional differences in funding regimes, governance structures, institutional practices, and socio-cultural variations. However, I argue that universities in the liberal states increasingly share some of the same institutional priorities because they are shaped by similar economic and political pressures. This chapter focuses on research that is based largely on political economy theories and discusses the current pressures on universities, including rising student enrolments, more diversity among students and faculty, the introduction of new technology, and rising operating costs relative to state funding. However, I focus on rising managerialism and corporatization, which includes expanded expectations by governing bodies of financial accountability, productivity, and international competitiveness.

The chapter begins with an overview of general labour market restructuring in the liberal states and proceeds to outline three aspects of university restructuring: changes in public funding, shifts in governance, and the strengthened focus on research. The rest of the chapter discusses university ranking systems and the increasing drive for international competitiveness. The gendered consequences of university restructuring, which are not always acknowledged in previous research, are noted throughout but are also discussed in more detail in Chapter 4 with findings from my own interviews.

Labour Market and Institutional Restructuring

Universities are commonly portrayed as ivory towers, but as workplaces they are influenced by many of the same pressures that have altered other work organizations over the past few decades. Especially since the mid-1980s, labour markets have been transformed, as governments in the liberal states entered into freer trade agreements with other governments and encouraged more international flow of capital and jobs. In addition, many governments deregulated aspects of their labour markets to accommodate these agreements and cut income taxes while raising consumption taxes. They also tightened eligibility for state income support and strengthened work incentives for welfare beneficiaries (Baker 2008; Banting and Beach 1995; Easton 2008; Fairbrother and Rainnie 2006; Lunt, O'Brien, and Stephens 2008; Vosko 2000, 2009).

The liberal states have typically allowed markets to operate with minimal state regulation, though Australia and New Zealand have historically been more interventionist than the others (Castles and Shirley

1996). However, compared to social democratic states (such as Sweden and Denmark), the liberal states have generally expected their citizens to rely on household earnings for economic well-being, offering relatively ungenerous support mainly to those who are already in financial need or family crisis (Esping-Andersen 1990; Kingfisher 2001; Scruggs and Allan 2006).

With freer trade, these liberal tendencies have been augmented as manufacturers and employers gained greater bargaining power by threatening to move capital, equipment, and labour offshore to countries with lower wages and operating costs. In addition, more work organizations began searching for experienced staff from other countries, as global labour markets developed for professional and managerial jobs. At the same time, technological changes have had a dual effect on workplaces: they have eliminated or down-skilled some positions but have also created new types of jobs while up-skilling others (Easton 2008; Torjman and Battle 1999).

A consequence of these developments is that, since the 1960s, diminishing numbers of employees in the liberal states enjoy job protection afforded by labour regulations or collective agreements (Banting and Beach 1995). In addition, more employment agreements are based on individual contracts or enterprise bargaining that governs only one workplace rather than on centralized bargaining that governs the entire industry (Fairbrother and Rainnie 2006). Second, a greater percentage of employees work in service-sector positions rather than primary industry or manufacturing (Easton 2008; Vosko 2009). Third, more workers find themselves in low-paid part-time or temporary (contingent) positions, and a greater percentage have become self-employed or actively engaged in raising funds to cover their wages or employment expenses (Kingfisher 2001; Vosko 2000).

The trend toward more part-time temporary and low-paid work has been called the "feminization of work," not only because more employees are women but also because the conditions in more jobs resemble those associated with women's work of a few decades ago (Armstrong and Armstrong 2010). In addition, more staff who prefer full-time positions are forced to accept fewer hours with less job security, although students and mothers with preschool children often seek temporary or part-time

Table 3.1   Total expenditure on research and development in higher education as % of gross domestic product

Country	% spent on research and development
Australia	–
Canada	.63
New Zealand	.36
United Kingdom	.44
United States	.36

Source: Extracted from CAUT (2011a, 57).

jobs. Furthermore, the qualifications for some permanent positions have been upgraded as job markets become more competitive and internationalized.

Since the 1980s, governments in the liberal states have become more concerned about curbing public spending, reducing public debt, and lowering income taxes. Consequently, they have required greater accountability from publicly funded institutions while also expecting increases in productivity (Easton 2008). In these countries, governments have typically viewed the knowledge economy as an important forum for the development of national productivity and international competitiveness, although they have not always been prepared to increase their funding to universities (Geiger 2004; Metcalfe 2010; Walby et al. 2007). Table 3.1 displays total expenditures on research and development in higher education as a percentage of gross domestic product.[1] These figures are similar in three of the liberal states, though data are missing for Australia. In addition, this table shows that expenditure in Canada is the highest in these countries.

As pressures on public resources grow, governments expect greater value for their grants to postsecondary education, more financial contributions from outside universities, and better student preparation for the job market. In addition, publicly funded universities are increasingly required to manage their state funds more effectively (Fletcher et al. 2007; Marginson and Considine 2000). These expectations have been placed on universities at a time when student enrolment, operating costs, and demand for new services such as equity and family-friendly programs are all increasing.

Restructuring the Funding for Postsecondary Education

State transfers to postsecondary institutions have always varied in value by jurisdiction, institutional type, and the political environment. For many years, publicly funded universities have received government grants based largely on student enrolments (or "bums on seats"). As enrolments rise, some governments are now developing new funding strategies and formulas. These include capping or limiting the number of students they are willing to fund each year, providing resources for student completion of degrees rather than enrolments, and offering additional funding for graduate and/or international students. They may also base a component of funding on the research productivity of academics (Fisher et al. 2009; Turk 2000).

In many jurisdictions, state contributions to university resources have not kept pace with increasing student enrolments or rising operating costs. In Chapter 1, I noted that Canadian government funding as a percentage of university operating revenue declined from 84 percent in 1978 to 58 percent in 2008 (CAUT 2011a, 2). However, these figures varied considerably by province. In Ontario, provincial government transfers to colleges and universities per equivalent full-time student diminished by 31.6 percent from 1992 to 2004, but Quebec actually increased transfers by 6.1 percent over the same period (Fisher et al. 2009). The general trend in the liberal states, however, is for state funding to drop relative to university operating costs.

To compensate, most universities have expanded their fundraising activities, and many now seek donations from alumni, former and current staff, and corporate donors for new buildings, scholarships, and other academic ventures (Mohrman, Ma, and Baker 2008; Slaughter and Leslie 1999). They have increased domestic tuition fees when permitted by governments, although this measure has not compensated for the shortfall in state funds. They have recruited more international students, and out-of-state students in the United States, charging them higher tuition fees. They have also attempted to attract students who receive the highest government grants, which usually includes graduate research students and those studying science, engineering, or medicine rather than the humanities and social sciences, where many women students and academics are located.

In New Zealand, for example, governments pay higher grants for doctoral students than for other students, and international students once paid higher tuition fees. However, some universities in that country are now attempting to attract more overseas doctoral students by charging them the (lower) domestic fees. Government discourse has assumed that these students will contribute to national research and development, and universities have accepted this argument. However, they also hope that more doctoral students will raise their research profile and thereby improve their reputation. In addition, they expect that more doctoral students and fewer undergraduates will lead to larger state grants, as doctoral students are funded at a higher level.

The changing proportion of public and private funding in the postsecondary sector is shown in Table 3.2 for the liberal states. This table reveals that funding from public sources is well below the OECD average in all these countries and has declined since 2000 except in the United States. With its many private universities and heavy reliance on private foundations, the United States has funded postsecondary education at the lowest level, but public funding has actually increased slightly since 2000. However, the trend toward decreasing public funding is evident in the other countries (although some data are missing for New Zealand). Government funding generally varies according to the philosophy of the political party in power and by the activities of national interest groups. Nordic countries continue to fund postsecondary institutions more generously, but most liberal states now receive a larger proportion of funding from private sources than in past decades (CAUT 2011a, 57).

I have already noted that universities deal with rising operating costs by saving money on salaries, hiring more part-time or contractually limited staff. This increase in part-time positions is particularly notable in the United States, where they rose from 30.2 percent of faculty in 1975 to 46.3 percent in 2003, while full-time non-tenure-track positions (contractually limited) increased from 13.0 percent to 18.7 percent of faculty (West and Curtis 2006, 7). Part-time or temporary lecturers are less expensive than permanent (or tenure-stream and tenured) academics

Table 3.2 Proportion of public and private funding in the postsecondary sector

	Public Sources		Private Sources	
Country	2006	2000	2006	2000
Australia	47.6	51.0	52.4	49.0
Canada	53.4	61.0	46.6	39.0
New Zealand	63.0	–	37.0	–
United Kingdom	64.8	67.7	35.2	32.3
United States	34.0	31.1	66.0	68.9
OECD average	72.6	77.7	27.4	22.2

Source: Extracted from CAUT (2011a, 57, Table 8.8).

because they are often paid for only one academic course or for one activity rather than for teaching, research, and service. In addition, part-time and contractual lecturers are sometimes paid only during teaching times and do not receive an annual salary, or they are remunerated for a fixed term, such as one semester or one to two years.

Hiring a greater percentage of temporary staff tends to create a flexible but dual labour market, especially if managers use them to teach large undergraduate classes while freeing up permanent and more senior academics to create knowledge. In the United States, for example, the number of full-time tenure-track positions has declined since the 1970s, until by 2007, 70 percent of full-time faculty held non-tenure-track, contractually limited, or contingent jobs. Most of these positions are teaching-intensive, receiving lower salaries and fewer employment-related benefits; a disproportionate number are filled by women (AAUP 2010).

To increase private funding, universities have encouraged their permanent academics to seek partnerships for their research projects and to apply for external funding rather than relying solely on internal university resources. Scholars might find research partnerships with university-based colleagues in other places or with community agencies, non-government organizations, or private industry. External funding could also come from publicly funded granting agencies, such as the Australian Research Council, the Social Sciences and Humanities

Research Council in Canada, the Marsden Fund in New Zealand, the Economic and Social Research Council in the United Kingdom, and the National Science Foundation in the United States. They could also accept research contracts from government departments, private corporations, foundations, or unions. Research partnerships with industry or government have sometimes led to scientific breakthroughs but also to apprehensions about academic freedom or controversies about confidential data, conflicts of interest, or even the credibility of findings.

Government concerns about managing budgets have also encouraged broader institutional restructuring within the postsecondary sector. This includes merging colleges of advanced education and teachers' colleges with existing universities and transforming some polytechnic institutes into universities of technology, often designed to make them more cost-effective. Consequently, many universities have become more engaged in vocational teaching than in the 1970s (Fletcher et al. 2007) and sometimes compete for state resources with other postsecondary providers, including private sector ones. In addition, restructuring has involved downsizing or closing departments that bring fewer students or lower resources to the university, or threatening to close entire institutions that appear to be mismanaging public funds (Larner and LeHeron 2005; Mohrman, Ma, and Baker 2008). However, changes in institutional governance are also apparent.

Governance and the Rise of Managerialism
In the liberal states, considerable research has focused on the governance of public universities and the ascent of managerialism as non-academic managers and administrators gain more control over university strategic goals and their implementation (Butterworth and Tarling 1994; Curtis and Matthewman 2005; Fisher et al. 2009; Larner and LeHeron 2005; Menzies and Newson 2008; Morley 2003; Peters and Roberts 1999; Turk 2000). In past decades, academics or former academics made many institutional decisions, with less assistance from professional administrators. Now, however, many public universities have altered their decision-making processes by adding corporate-style managers while reducing the extent of decision making by academics.

In the United Kingdom, for instance, the Higher Education Statistics Agency (HESA) found that the number of managers in universities increased by 33 percent from 2003 to 2009, but the number of academics and students increased only by 10 and 9 percent (Tahir 2010). Although some academics are also managers, HESA defines "manager" as a new type of non-academic professional involved in such activities as finance, marketing, human resources, student services, and quality assurance. The increase in managers has led to considerable academic concern about hyper-bureaucracy and diminishing academic freedom (ibid.), but it has also provided career paths for administrators within the university.

The expansion of managerial staff has both promoted gender equity and augmented the gender gap. Compared to academic staff, more administrative or general staff in universities are women, some of whom have been able to achieve promotion through the increase of middle-management positions. Furthermore, formalized rules created by the new managers, combined with committee decision making, have helped female academics and administrators to attain promotion by clarifying the rules and preventing bias and favouritism in decision making. However, the managerial university has hired more temporary teachers, many of whom are women. Academic managers have also devised new ways of measuring and monitoring productivity, and the academic gender gap has been perpetuated by higher expectations of research productivity (Baker 2009b; Currie, Thiele, and Harris 2002; Morley 2003; Reimer 2004; Sagaria 2007).

In some institutions, councils or the main decision-making bodies now contain members appointed by government, where they can monitor state investment. These new managerial practices have often been justified by budget shortfalls or crises that require decision-makers with a background in finance or corporate management (Geiger 2004; Menzies and Newson 2008). More universities have also adopted business-like or corporate practices, such as clarifying their key performance indicators, emphasizing auditing and cost cutting, and enhancing measures of productivity. However, many variations are evident. For example, most universities still permit faculty to take research leave or sabbaticals at regular intervals, but many no longer pay full salary during this leave.

Most continue to provide basic work equipment, such as computers and printers, whereas some ask academics to buy some of their own equipment, especially if they are able to acquire it with external research grants.

Many universities now compare their institutional statistics, or benchmark with other institutions, both within their own country and internationally (Brenneis, Shore, and Wright 2005; Taylor and Braddock 2007). These benchmarking exercises often focus on student statistics, such as staff-student ratios and state funding per equivalent full-time student (EFTS).[2] However, attention is also being paid to indicators of staff productivity, such as the total number of students taught by individual lecturers, publications per academic, and the amount of external research funding each one brings to the university (Currie, Thiele, and Harris 2002; Morley 2003).

Many universities have developed a culture of accountability, including a reliance on merit pay rather than automatic salary increases with seniority. University managers are also requiring academics to complete annual performance reviews, reporting all their professional activities in teaching, service/administration, and research. Some of these new measures of productivity and a greater reliance on merit have actually assisted hard-working female scholars to gain collegial recognition and promotion, especially those who were previously bypassed by heads or committees using unwritten rules (Luke 1997). Especially when productivity includes teaching and service duties, or counts the number of students taught, many women academics benefit. However, these kinds of accounting changes also require academics to spend more time documenting their professional achievements and activities, and their time spent on teaching, service, research, conferences, or annual leave.

Because universities have been using business-like management practices and emphasizing marketing, performance indicators, and private funding, they now resemble private corporations rather than public institutions that provide services to citizens (Fletcher et al. 2007; Morley 2003; Schuster and Finkelstein 2006). Nevertheless, many governments also expect public universities to teach more students, to share their research findings with the public, and to continue promoting the goals of teaching and research excellence (Menzies and Newson 2008).

The Rise of the Research University

Even before the restructuring of the 1980s and '90s, some universities gave a higher priority to research than to undergraduate teaching. Historically, the research universities expected their academics to create new knowledge, acquire competitive grants, and publish their findings in high-impact journals, as well as teaching undergraduates and supervising graduate students (Caplow and McGee 1958; Jencks and Riesman 1977). Now they have strengthened their efforts to market themselves as prestigious research institutions, attempting to attract internationally acclaimed researchers and hiring contract researchers to help these "stars" raise their productivity. Some universities are also admitting a higher percentage of graduate research students, using them as teaching assistants or temporary lecturers. Some may accept only the top undergraduate and graduate students who apply (Mohrman, Ma, and Baker 2009).

Managers are exerting even more pressure on academics to apply for competitive and external research grants, partly because they bring prestige to the university but also because these external funds help reduce the costs of doing research within the university. Furthermore, some granting agencies permit universities to retain a substantial percentage of the external grant as overheads to help pay for operating costs, including space, electricity, and equipment.

In contrast, many teaching universities continue to concentrate on classroom instruction, teaching and learning, and providing undergraduate students with a general education. Fewer expectations have been placed on their teaching staff to train future researchers or to head research projects and write articles and books themselves. In addition, the teaching universities tend to hire more women academics than the research universities (CAUT 2009; Fletcher et al. 2007; New Zealand Human Rights Commission 2008). However, they also expect their academics to spend more time on classroom teaching and teaching-related activities.

Some of the colleges or polytechnic institutes that have become universities now pressure their teaching staff to obtain doctorates, develop new research projects, and publish their findings. However, they also expect them to teach more hours per week or more classes per year than their colleagues at the research universities. Generally, rapid changes in the teaching universities mean that recently hired academics have higher research qualifications than existing staff. Because new recruits are more likely to have earned doctorates and to publish in refereed journals, they tend to receive faster promotion, which can lead to resentments among more established teaching staff (Thomas and Davies 2002).

New electronic procedures for academic job applications tend to facilitate submissions from around the world. With increasing numbers of international applications, many universities have raised their entry qualifications, expecting new recruits to have completed doctorates, teaching experience, and peer-reviewed publications at the time of hiring. The prestigious doctoral universities are particularly able to sustain these expectations as they typically receive many international applications for each advertised vacancy. At the same time, already employed academics without doctorates are pushed to obtain this qualification as soon as possible or risk the redundancy, denial of promotion, or pressure for early retirement.

The current competitive university environment tends to reward individuals with scholarly confidence and entrepreneurial skills who are willing and able to develop large-scale projects with international collaborators and external funding. However, a number of studies have found that women's projects tend to be smaller in scale, more applied and local, and that they more often rely on qualitative research, feminist theories, and female subjects and collaborators (Knights and Richards 2003; Leahey 2006, 2007; Long 2001; Wyn, Acker, and Richards 2000). Given this, male colleagues are less likely to read women's published work or attend their conference presentations. Furthermore, senior academics who often exert disproportionate influence in promotion decisions and research assessment are likely to be men. These gendered patterns contribute to women's lower visibility as productive scholars and potential collaborators with men, but collaboration has become more consequential in the present university environment (Fletcher et al. 2007).

Academics and their managers often focus on the "impact factor" of research and publications, including citations of research publications by other academics, favourable reviews of their books, and research leading to patents or policy changes. Hiring research stars can raise the standing of universities by attracting productive well-known academics who then attract high-quality graduate students. However, hiring research stars also tends to encourage a wider discrepancy between the status of teaching and research (Side and Robbins 2007).

In recent years, both teaching and research universities have been hiring research chairs with private bequests or new state resources. These individuals are expected to strengthen the institution's profile of funded research, peer-reviewed publications, and international collaboration. However, most chairs are given to men because they already occupy about 80 percent of the senior academic positions. In Canada, 83.5 percent of the tier one Canada research chairs (for full professors) and 68.8 percent of the tier two chairs (for intermediate-level scholars) have been awarded to men (CAUT 2009). In addition, many government-funded chairs in the Canada Research Chair Program were located in science (which has a disproportionate number of male academics), and many did not have to be openly advertised (Grant and Drakich 2010; Side and Robbins 2007). In their 2004 interviews with Canada research chair holders, Grant and Drakich (2011) concluded that when they were given equal levels of institutional support and prestige, they performed in the same manner. However, more women hold tier two chairs, which are accompanied by fewer resources and less prestige. Moreover, the pressure to produce research and publications is high for occupants of these positions, a particularly challenging situation for women with daily care responsibilities.

Both governments and public universities are becoming more concerned about the productivity and the national and international reputation of postsecondary institutions. Consequently, government-related agencies have developed research assessment exercises in some liberal states to rank universities on various measures of research productivity. Non-government ranking systems also exist, such as the Times Higher Education–QS World University Rankings discussed later in this chapter. These systems typically include a wide variety of measures to indicate the quality of universities, many of which are debatable (Mohrman, Ma, and Baker 2008; Taylor and Braddock 2007). However, the state-sponsored systems remain the focus in the rest of this chapter.

National Research Assessment Exercises

In recent years, the differences between research and teaching universities have been altered by national research evaluation exercises; in some cases they have been augmented, and in other ways they have become blurred. Canada and the United States have not introduced these systems as education falls under the jurisdiction of the provinces and states, and an assessment system would be politically difficult or impossible at the national level. However, the other three liberal states have introduced national research evaluation exercises, and their outcomes influence resource allocations from the state to the universities.

The United Kingdom's system, previously called the Research Assessment Exercise (RAE) and now reconfigured as the Research Excellence Framework (REF), evaluates the research outputs of university departments or academic units. Australia's Research Quality Framework (RQF), which also appraised academic units, has recently been replaced by a new system called Excellence in Research for Australia (ERA). New Zealand's Performance-Based Research Fund (PBRF) assesses individual academics as well as units and entire universities, and will be discussed in more detail below because it provides useful background for the 2008 interviews.

Historically, state funding to universities and colleges in New Zealand was based largely on student enrolments, but in the 1990s, the conservative National Party government encouraged the accreditation of private postsecondary providers and new programs of study. It also introduced tuition fees instead of full state funding of postsecondary education but developed a student loan system that made education more accessible to people from lower-income households (Larner and LeHeron 2005). These policies contributed to rising postsecondary student enrolments, which then forced the government to increase its financial contributions to a level that it perceived to be unacceptably high.

Consequently, a new system of funding postsecondary or tertiary research – the Performance-Based Research Fund (PBRF) – was devised in New Zealand by the Tertiary Education Commission (TEC). Implemented in 2002 by the Labour-led government, it added a 20 percent component of competitive funding for research while abolishing the former enrolment-based grants for research (but retained them for teaching). The political discourse surrounding the PBRF exercise was that it was designed to encourage and reward excellence, but it is also a funding mechanism to differentiate between research and teaching institutions in a climate of rising costs and the perception of scarce public resources. I use the word "perception" because income tax rates were reduced in the 1990s by the National government, and the proliferation of private education providers was encouraged, contributing to the shortage of public funds.

The PBRF system ranks the research productivity of individual academics and their institutions, and has been used by managers to encourage higher levels of productivity without necessarily raising salaries. For this reason, it could be seen as an example of increasing neo-liberal restructuring (Curtis and Matthewman 2005). PBRF initially provided state grants to universities, polytechnic institutes, and colleges, although some institutes and colleges have now opted out. However, the system continues to focus on the research productivity scores of individual scholars working in universities, as well as postgraduate degree completions and external research income.[3]

New Zealand's PBRF requires individual academics to report a confidential evidence portfolio to the TEC consisting of their research outputs and including justifications of the merit of their four best works (worth 70 percent of their score), their peer esteem (worth 15 percent), and their contribution to the research environment (worth 15 percent). In 2003 and 2006, these portfolios were assessed by a number of disciplinary-related panels of senior academics; most panel members (including myself) were based in New Zealand, but some were in the other liberal states. A third round of PBRF is scheduled for mid-2012.

The individual scores calculated by PBRF assessment panels are confidential and are later sent directly to the academics themselves but not to their department chairs/heads, university managers, or administrators. However, the TEC publicly discloses aggregate university scores based on various aspects of research productivity, such as the institution with the highest-ranked academics or those attracting the most external research funding, as well as scores for academic disciplines and units within universities (such as departments, schools, and centres).

Not surprisingly, university managers are using PBRF institutional scores for marketing purposes and their estimates of individual scores (garnered from departmental data) as performance indicators for their academic staff. They are also attempting to poach high-rated scholars from other New Zealand universities as well as hiring research stars from overseas to improve their university's future PBRF rating. Individual scholars have sometimes used their high scores to argue for promotion and salary increases or to gain new positions elsewhere. However, many have been critical of the process, especially those receiving low scores, and find it time consuming and stressful, which will be discussed later in this book.

Individual PBRF scores are created from the combined ratings for the quality of research outputs (focusing on peer-reviewed publications), peer esteem, and contribution to the research environment, with the highest weighting given to research outputs. Not surprisingly, men received the highest average scores, which roughly correlate with academic rank (Curtis, Phibbs, and Meager 2011; Middleton 2009; Ransley 2007). Furthermore, the academic standards used in this research evaluation exercise are similar to those applied in university promotion applications. Men's higher PBRF scores could also be attributed to their greater degree of research specialization, more theoretical and scientific areas of study, the stronger research culture in the male-dominated departments, and men's older average age and seniority, which provide opportunities to develop peer esteem and make a significant contribution to research.

In the PBRF exercise, individual scholars were given the opportunity to mention special circumstances that might have interfered with their research productivity. Many women reported caring responsibilities for children, sick or dying partners, and frail parents that hindered their research, whereas men were more likely to cite administrative responsibilities (such as department head or dean). In public discussions of PBRF, the gender balance of some assessment panels was criticized for over-representing male academics. Research suggests that male colleagues tend to grant lower value to feminist scholarship as well as to research relating to family, women, or gender (Leahey 2006). It also indicates that women are least likely to find permanent positions in institutions and departments that focus on research (Burris 2004; Long 2001; Monroe et al. 2008). All these factors could lower their PBRF scores.

Research evaluation exercises are usually designed to increase the quality and quantity of academic publications and funded projects, as well as to create new state funding mechanisms for postsecondary education. However, they tend to alter the shape and direction of academic disciplines by influencing what researchers study, how they study it, and how they disseminate their results. These exercises also shape the identities of academics, encouraging them to see themselves and to present themselves to university managers and colleagues as researchers rather than teachers or lecturers (Beck and Young 2005; Bernstein 2000; Middleton 2009; Sikes 2006).

Internationalization and University Ranking Systems

In recent decades, universities have become more international in their marketing, their attempts to garner new resources, and their recruitment of academics and students. They have developed overseas campuses to attract more students and have created official exchange programs with other universities for teaching and new ventures relating to research and administration (Chan and Fisher 2008). In addition, they have developed associations of like-minded universities in particular regions or that espouse similar strategic goals.

With greater institutional competition, non-government ranking systems have also been developed to compare the quality of universities, both nationally and internationally (Fletcher et al. 2007; Morley 2003; Taylor and Braddock 2007). For example, all the liberal states have participated in the Times Higher Education–QS World University Rankings. This system is normally revised annually and has relied on a variety of indicators. Half of the score has been reputational, based on peer reviews from academics and employers about the statuses of universities. In addition, the system has included measures of faculty-student ratios, faculty citations, percentage of international faculty, and the proportion of international students. There is considerable debate about these indicators, what they actually measure, and how they are compiled.[4]

We need to keep in mind that because the various ranking instruments do not use a standardized measure, they can produce dissimilar scores for the same university (Taylor and Braddock 2007). The Shanghai Jiao Tong University ranking system, for example, is based largely on

research-related prizes won by alumni as well as academic staff, on publications by current faculty in specific scientific journals, citations of
their work, and various measures of institutional size (ibid.). This suggests
that universities with strong science, medical, and engineering schools
that emphasize scientific research would rank higher on this scale than
those focusing on the humanities or social sciences (where more women
scholars are typically employed).

In ranking systems based largely on reputation, the more established
universities tend to receive the highest scores, as they have decades or
centuries of scholarship, funded research, alumni, and corporate donors.
This implies that university rankings partly reinforce past priorities and
reputations. However, some newer institutions have made rapid gains
within ranking systems by hiring productive researchers and paying
them high salaries, building new facilities with the latest research equipment (sometimes assisted by government grants), and developing effective marketing strategies to increase graduate student enrolments and
to attract research-active staff.

As university managers focus more on international standing and
performance, they gradually alter the academic working environment.
In order to gain job security or promotion to the next rank, academics
must spend more time justifying their performance and productivity.
This may include their teaching effectiveness and service contributions
to the institution and/or community. However, the emphasis on international standing and performance often focuses on academics' success
in attracting research money, the quantity and quality of their research
outputs, and the impact of their research on stakeholders. Those with
international networks and reputations tend to be viewed more favourably and become better remunerated (Butterworth and Tarling 1994;
Curtis and Matthewman 2005; Peters and Roberts 1999; Thomas and
Davies 2002).

Employees always face competing demands on their time and energy,
which sometimes produce stress that spills over to their personal lives
(Kinman and Jones 2004). Many academics, including the participants
in the 2008 New Zealand study, stated that growing managerial practices
interfered with scholarship because they involved time-consuming documentation of work activities. They also required the careful development

of compelling arguments about the contribution that one's scholarship and publications had made to the institution and discipline. Women have not always made these kinds of arguments as well as men have (Probert 2005).

Institutional Support for Gender Equity

Since the 1960s, university managers have acknowledged that some categories of students and employees need additional support to succeed, but equity initiatives have varied substantially by jurisdiction and institution. Bursaries and scholarships have been established to assist able but low-income students and disadvantaged minorities to complete their degrees. Governments instigated student loan systems, such as the Canada Student Loan Scheme established in 1964 and the New Zealand scheme in the 1980s (Baker 1975, 6; Larner and LeHeron 2005). Some governments have also created employment equity programs to urge employers to expand opportunities for female applicants, as well as those from minority backgrounds or with various disabilities, as the Canadian government did in the 1980s.

In the 1970s, after considerable lobbying by women's groups, some governments, universities, and professional associations set up committees to study the status of women. For example, the Royal Commission on the Status of Women in Canada reported its findings in 1970 (Royal Commission 1970). In addition, the late 1960s and early 1970s marked the beginning of feminist scholarship and women's studies in Canada (Robbins et al. 2008). An Academic Women's Association had just been established at the Canadian university where I completed my 1973 study, and shortly afterward the university senate created a Task Force on the Status of Women. These two organizations helped raise awareness of the lower average salaries of academic women and sex discrimination on this campus.

In recent decades, more universities have acknowledged the existence of harassment, bullying, and power imbalances inherent in supervisory and employment relationships. Many have formulated policies and procedures to govern student and staff behaviour, to investigate allegations of harassment, and to discipline those proven to be involved. However, reports of discrimination and sexual harassment continue in women's stories about their university experiences, although alleged incidents now seem more subtle. One continuing problem is that close mentoring relationships between a senior man and a woman student are sometimes misperceived as sexual in nature, and the woman is accused of sleeping her way to the top (Fletcher et al. 2007). Separated or divorced women, who are over-represented among academic women, most commonly report sexual harassment. More reports also come from older women discussing their past experiences, implying some positive change over time (Carr et al. 2000; Rosser 2004).

Some institutions have also established special mentoring programs for students and staff. For students, these have been based largely on ethnicity and low income, but for staff they have focused on gender and leadership potential. Initiatives that have proven popular with female academics in Australia and New Zealand include gender-based mentoring, which matches junior women with successful senior women who are willing to share their time and knowledge of institutional practices. Networking programs have also attempted to introduce women academic and administrative staff to female colleagues in the same organization, job category, or profession, encouraging them to discuss collective challenges and successful strategies to overcome them. In addition, universities have established paid parental leave, campus childcare services, and work-life balance programs that permit employees to work more flexible hours. Programs comprising both men and women have also been created in some jurisdictions for academics who are interested in leadership or senior management positions, including mentoring for future heads of department or senior leadership positions.

Although the effectiveness of gender-based equity programs is difficult to evaluate, the participants themselves often provide positive feedback. Female scholars say that they particularly benefit from networking with other academic women, which makes them feel more integrated or accepted in a male-dominated profession (Gibson 2006; Hartley and Dobele 2009). However, initiatives such as women's mentoring and work-life balance programs are not always well resourced or viewed as integral components of the mission of the institution (Gibson 2006; Kosoko-Lasaki, Sonnino, and Voytko 2006; Le Feuvre 2009). Gerdes (2003) argues that to really make a difference, senior women may need to use their position to help the university culture become more congenial to female academics, especially those who are young mothers.

University equity committees and women's committees also provide vehicles through which a dialogue on gender equality and equity can occur. However, a study by Wilson, Gadbois, and Nichol (2008) found that only 40 percent of Canadian universities have equality-related committees, and only 34 percent have status of women committees through their faculty associations. American research found that academic managers expressed concern about gender equity, but status of women reports were not always accessible to the public, and the structures to implement systemic changes were largely absent (Bird, Litt, and Wang 2004).

Several studies report a backlash against family-friendly and affirmative action programs in the managerial university (Drakich and Stewart 2007; Thomas and Davies 2002). They reveal that some employees are afraid to use family-related leave for fear of losing professional credibility, and that mothers with young children are particularly concerned about the heightened productivity requirements in the current work environment.

Conclusion

In recent decades, public universities have accepted more female graduate students and academics, but at the same time they restructured to deal with rising operating costs, new funding and accountability regimes, and more competition for faculty and students. This has meant that they have increased their commitment to some of the very priorities and practices that contribute to the gender gap, such as augmenting the dual labour market by hiring more research stars (often males) while expecting temporary or junior staff (disproportionately women) to teach the larger undergraduate classes.

In addition, they are placing more pressure on academics to apply for competitive grants, deliver papers at international conferences, accept visiting professorships at other universities, develop collaborative partnerships, increase their research output, and perform more administrative tasks formerly done by administrators. Although both men and women have excelled in these activities, they require different skills than classroom teaching, more time and commitment, and in the case of international travel, more household resources and family support. A competitive environment and university downsizing can stress all academics, but recently hired staff without job security and those deemed to be low research performers are most likely to fear lack of promotion or redundancy. Women in the liberal states form a disproportionate percentage of new, part-time, and temporary academics, with fewer peer-reviewed publications (Nakhaie 2007; Side and Robbins 2007; Thomas and Davies 2002).

Some researchers have also argued that "feminized fields," which have focused less on research, have been disproportionately retrenched (Curtis 2005). Departments recently closed or merged in New Zealand include women's studies, European languages, education, and social work, all of which are characterized by a high percentage of women and low research outputs (Baker 2009b). In Canada, women's studies departments have been merged in recent years, but many other departments have experienced redundancies in the liberal states.

Some university redundancies are "voluntary," but older women seem to be more willing than older men to work part-time or to take early retirement. They are especially amenable to reducing their working hours if it means that younger colleagues will retain their jobs and if their own (usually older) partners have already retired (Tizard and Owen 2001). As universities experience tighter budgets and hiring is restricted, the possibility of redressing the gender imbalance becomes less likely, especially as older academics are retiring later (Acker and Armenti 2004).

Universities have always rewarded academics who are willing and able to devote long hours to the profession, to publish widely, and to remain fully employed throughout their careers (Bernard 1964; Caplow and McGee 1958; Jencks and Riesman 1977). Under these rules of the game, more male academics reach the top of the profession while many women flounder in the junior and middle ranks.

Social Capital and Gendered Responses to University Practices

4

Women have difficulty moving into a male domain ... There is an unconscious camaraderie, involving informal decision-making, and it's hard for women to break into this.

– FEMALE ASSISTANT PROFESSOR, CANADA, 1973

It's a bit of an old adage ... that women ... have to work twice as hard with a quarter of the support, and you just know that if you take on a senior role like head of school or head of department that you are going to have far more trouble from people than you would if you were a bloke.

– FEMALE PROFESSOR, NEW ZEALAND, 2008

This chapter is the first of three to examine the contributors to the academic gender gap by drawing on my qualitative interviews in Canada and New Zealand as well as the wider research to show that though the gender gap in "social capital" has declined considerably over the decades, differences nevertheless remain. Social capital is sometimes divided into "hard" and "soft" forms: the former is said to develop from instrumental ties, such as knowing the "right" people or having the ability to acquire the necessary information and resources to gain promotion. The latter springs from expressive ties or supportive relationships that contribute to feelings of belonging or job satisfaction (van Emmerik 2006). Research suggests that access to both forms of social capital in academia tends to vary by gender (Burris 2004; M. Fox 2005; Lim and Herrer-Sobek 2000; Monroe et al. 2008).

Gaining Academic Qualifications

In Chapter 2, we saw that more females than males now obtain undergraduate degrees, but males are still more likely to complete a doctorate in most liberal states and to specialize in disciplines leading to lucrative jobs. Females tend to focus on the humanities, social sciences, and education, which contribute to lower employment rates and salaries (Auriol 2007; CAUT 2011a). Male academics are also more likely to have a PhD as their highest qualification when they accept their first full-time university position (Brooks 1997; Nakhaie 2007). Those with doctorates have already proven they can do research, are more likely to identify as researchers, and tend to publish more than academics with lower degrees (Monroe et al. 2008).

Teaching universities tend to be less stringent than research universities about hiring doctorate holders or applicants graduating from prestigious universities. They typically have a lower percentage of academics with PhDs but also a higher percentage of women scholars (Fletcher et al. 2007; Leathwood and Read 2008). In both kinds of universities, departments such as social work, education, business, and law place less emphasis on the doctorate because they also value practical experience to enhance the relevance of their qualification to future employers. However, more departments and universities now expect recently hired individuals to arrive with a doctorate or to complete one as soon as possible.

The eminence of the university where academics received their highest degree or previously worked remains an important indicator of scholarly worth and social capital (Burris 2004; Lamont 2009). A rough pecking order exists among universities, bolstered by the systems of assessment and ranking discussed in Chapter 3. When research universities hire junior academics, they often prefer graduates from high-profile universities such as Oxford or Harvard, but not everyone has the opportunity or ability to attend prominent graduate schools. Educational sociologists continue to emphasize the statistical association between social class background and institutional affiliation/educational achievement (Reay at al. 2001; Van De Werfhorst, Sullivan, and Cheung 2003).

Academic Qualifications: 1973

During the 1970s, the vast majority of PhDs were earned by men, and assumptions about appropriate gender roles and men's greater need for funding impeded women's pursuit of a doctorate. In my 1973 interviews (based on a purposive sample of academic women at a large university in western Canada), an assistant professor with a temporary appointment in the humanities reported that she had been told by her doctoral supervisor that he would have recommended her for a Woodrow Wilson Fellowship if she were a man. However, he assumed that she would not get it because of her gender and therefore did not bother to write the letter of recommendation (Baker 1975, 172).

Other participants stated that they had been encouraged by parents and teachers to continue their graduate education but not always with the intention of developing lifetime careers. Several seemed to make idiosyncratic career choices (Epstein 1971), such as the social sciences doctoral student who said that she applied for a PhD just "to shut up" her friends and professors who were constantly urging her to continue her studies on the basis of her previous scholarly success (Baker 1975, 172). A lecturer in education said that both she and her husband had been studying law, but they decided that one of them should be earning some money: "So I went to teachers college and became a teacher" (ibid., 174). Later, she found work in the education faculty despite her initial interest in law.

Most of the women in the 1973 study reported that their parents and teachers had encouraged them to develop their intellect, but they initially entered female-dominated professions rather than moving directly into male-dominated university jobs. Fifteen of the thirty-nine interviewees began their careers as schoolteachers (ibid.). One indicated that her parents were from a middle-class background in which "girls became

nurses and got married" (ibid., 158). However, she had a "burning ambition" since childhood to become a lawyer, so after studying home economics, switching to education, and teaching for four years, she finally
began studying law.

Academic Qualifications: 2008

Now the gender distribution of new doctorates has almost equalized
in the liberal states, but about 80 percent of senior academic positions
are still held by males. In the 2008 interviews (carried out in two New
Zealand universities), academic qualifications differed less by gender
than by type of university, partly because the sample included only
academics with PhDs and permanent positions. More participants from
the research university had achieved doctorates from prestigious overseas
universities, won international scholarships (such as the Commonwealth
Scholarship), and taught in other countries.

The experience of completing an overseas doctorate was not always
positive for all interviewees. For example, a senior female professor from
the research university mentioned that her doctorate was gained in
Australia during the late 1970s, when many PhD supervisors came from
the United Kingdom. When I asked her if she had ever published or
joint-authored conference papers with her thesis supervisors, she replied,
"Gosh no. My supervisors were fairly remote ... When I gave [my principal
supervisor] draft chapters to read, he would say 'carry on old chap' ... I
didn't really have any effective supervision for that PhD at all, which is
in part why it took me rather a long time to complete it because I was
teaching at the time."

Participants from the teaching university were more likely to have
local doctorates (often from the research university) and local teaching
experience. More of them completed their PhDs later in life, after working in another occupation or teaching for years in the teaching institution
before it became a university. In addition, more participants from this
university were women, and more reported working-class backgrounds,
lower career expectations, and less support from family and mentors.

Some bright and ambitious students from low-income families win
bursaries and scholarships, and continue their education to the highest
levels. However, studies from the sociology of education show that young

people from well-off families with educated parents continue to enjoy greater opportunities to graduate from distinguished universities (Burris 2004; Rothstein 2004). This suggests that education contributes to the social reproduction of a stratified society (Bourdieu 1977), with some of this stratification perpetuated by universities.

Academic Mentoring

Gender socialization, gender regulation, and gendered practices persist in schools and universities, although to a lesser extent than in the 1970s. Male children and youth are still more likely than females to be perceived as future lifelong earners and are therefore offered greater support to pursue professional careers (Connell 1995, 2000; Nayak and Kehily 2008). Young men tend to be given more inside information about workplace practices, which provides opportunities to engage in occupational planning, to develop work-related skills, and to gain professional confidence. Despite few gender differences in new doctoral degrees, young men have been found to plan more ambitious careers and express stronger intentions to reach the top of the employment hierarchy, earn high salaries, and take on leadership positions (Fels 2004; Probert 2005).

Effective mentoring has been related to access to insider knowledge, higher research productivity, promotional success, and career satisfaction in academia (Brooks 1997; Kosoko-Lasaki, Sonnino, and Voytko 2006). Not surprisingly, studies find that more men than women say that their doctoral experience was positive, their supervisors were interested in their research, and that they had co-published with them (Carr et al. 2000; Gibson 2006; Seagram, Gould, and Pyke 1998). Supervisors and other faculty sometimes believe that male students are more committed to their careers because they speak more enthusiastically and openly about their employment plans. Men's apparent career commitment attracts sponsorship, which then helps to broaden professional networks in early career (Probert 2005; White 2004).

Mentoring and Role Models: 1973

Researchers in the 1970s used the concept of sponsored mobility to emphasize the importance of mentoring for students to complete a doctorate, find an academic job, and gain subsequent promotions

(Patterson 1971). In my 1973 interviews, many subjects reported that they held traditional employment aspirations when they were younger and had assumed that they would move into a traditional female profession until a teacher or professor encouraged them to raise their aspirations. For example, one temporary lecturer said, "I had always planned on being a nurse or a teacher, as I thought that these were my only alternatives ... At the end of my sophomore year [at an American university], a senior professor ... convinced me that I was 'too good' for education, and that I should go instead for a BA ... I was then thinking in terms of teaching prep school or in a liberal arts college – but didn't consider a PhD. I don't know why." After teaching for two years in an American women's college, she decided to gain a doctorate. Otherwise, she said, "I would be stuck at this level forever" (Baker 1975, 158).

Few interviewees reported linear career paths in which they intended to become an academic at the beginning of their doctoral studies. Because the sample lacked male comparisons, we cannot be sure that males chose linear career paths at that time either. Nevertheless, some of the women's stories seemed rather gendered: a social sciences doctoral student had not planned to go to university but said that her headmistress "dared me to apply for Oxford and Cambridge, because she knew I would not refuse such a challenge" (ibid., 171). After being accepted and eventually graduating from Cambridge, the participant continued for a PhD "because my advisor felt that one of her students should go on to graduate school. I was the choice, as the other girl was getting married" (ibid.). Several other women talked about drifting into academic careers after being shoulder-tapped by a senior academic or becoming disillusioned with "female" jobs.

Absence of suitable role models has often been advanced as one explanation for the gender gap, but my interviews showed that female students did not always view academic women as positive models. In the 1973 interviews, a former doctoral student in science, who had recently withdrawn from her program, implied when she spoke of her former thesis supervisor that the available role models were discouraging: "She always came in very early in the morning and worked late hours. She took work home every single night, despite the fact that she had two small children to care for. But she was promoted at a slower rate than her male colleagues and received less pay. I could see myself being overburdened as my supervisor was ... After I get a PhD and work for a number of years – that could be me – if I'm lucky!" (ibid., 163). With the shortage of constructive role models, many interviewees saw themselves as atypical or deviant in their desire to become academics. At the same time, many also saw their housewife mothers as negative role models and hoped to develop more rewarding and challenging occupational lives.

These comments about suitable role models resonate with my personal experience as a graduate student. When I began my doctoral studies in 1972, thirty faculty members worked full-time in the Sociology Department of the University of Alberta, but none were women. In addition, very few were Canadian-born, which suggests that even in the 1970s many academics working in Canada had crossed international borders to find employment. My doctoral study sprang from my curiosity about the experiences of academic women; I wanted to become an academic but did not personally know any female scholars.

Epstein (1971) argued that attrition rates have always been higher for early-career women because they encounter less mentoring and support for graduate education, a certain amount of dependency training from parents and partners, more pressure to concentrate on family responsibilities, and fewer female role models. All these factors were evident in my 1973 study. As one doctoral student explained, "It is easier for women graduate students to quit. It's a socially acceptable option. People say they've come back to 'normal'" (Baker 1975, 236).

Mentoring and Role Models: 2008

In the New Zealand interviews, only half of the thirty participants reported that they had received any significant mentoring during graduate studies or their early career. Again, more differences were apparent between the two universities than between men and women, or even between those in junior or senior positions. For example, a female lecturer and scholarship student from the research university spoke of the male academic who had encouraged her to pursue a doctorate and academic career: "[He] was very much a mentor figure for me and was really the one who was responsible for saying 'You can do a PhD,' which I hadn't even really thought about, 'and this is how you do it.'" A male lecturer from the research university, who came from a privileged background, spoke of his many mentors: "I got two really good scholarships. My parents [also encouraged me to do a doctorate]. They're both academics ... I had a number of mentors. I had lots of people encouraging me to do a PhD – *expecting* me to do a PhD." Participants who reported the strongest mentoring relationships were scholarship winners from the research university with high-achieving parents.

In contrast, interviewees who claimed to have no mentor were more likely to work at the teaching university, to come from working-class backgrounds with less educated parents, to mention disputes with supervisors, or to suggest that their doctorate took "too long" to complete (from the supervisor's and their viewpoint). For instance, a female lecturer from the teaching university, who took twelve years to finish her PhD, said, "I lost my way a little – I mean, I just went off on a tangent ... I was a fairly shy student and I wonder if I could have been more forthcoming about my needs as a student to the supervisor ... Financially, I don't come from a wealthy family, you know, and I was always working." Research also suggests that female doctoral students who become pregnant or already have babies are least likely to be mentored into academic positions (Bracken, Allen, and Dean 2006; Lynch 2008). This finding was reinforced by a mother from a junior position at the teaching university who recalled her doctoral experiences in another country: "I certainly ran into conflict with my supervisor, especially towards the end, which I know that he wrote off as me being pregnant and hormonal."

Women in the 2008 study also talked about lack of positive role models, usually meaning senior academics who were also married mothers. Most spoke about male role models, such as a female lecturer from the teaching university, who said, "Actually when it comes to role models, it was often the males that sort of were encouraging ... especially the younger ones and the more liberal ones that sort of said go for it. If I look back, I didn't really have female role models ... A lot of [women academics] came through the glass ceiling and quite a lot of them had the attitude that, you know, I made it the hard way so therefore you will make it the hard way. So the support was sometimes more forthcoming from some of the males." Although some women and men talked about positive female role models, a young mother at the research university expressed a typical female concern when she said, "Some of my biggest role models in terms of inspiration to do the job were men, but one of the things I have been looking for is role models of women who've had families and been successful in academia. I've been trying to seek some of those people out but sometimes have been discouraged by their experiences and the difficulties they've faced."

In the wider literature, lack of positive female role models is seen as a contributor to higher attrition rates among women graduate students and junior academics (Bracken, Allen, and Dean 2006; Long 2001). In both my studies, despite the fact that they were decades apart and took place in different countries, the women participants saw few happily married mothers working in senior university positions and were often uninspired by high-ranking women who were single or childless. Therefore, lack of positive role models seems to be one of the enduring contributors to the academic gender gap.

Hiring Practices and Job Location

In the present competitive climate, universities often hire junior academics from an international pool of applicants, preferring those with published articles and previous teaching experience. They have invested considerable time and energy developing universal and impersonal criteria for hiring and promotion, but particularism, favouritism, and cronyism have always existed in the professions, and they continue today (Bagilhole and Goode 2001; Lamont 2009). Academics regularly shoulder-tap their like-minded colleagues at other universities and urge them to apply for positions in their department before they are formally advertised, providing them with inside information and lobbying departmental colleagues to favour these candidates.

For many scholars, searching for new recruits who are known to them is preferable to hiring strangers because the candidates' personalities and capabilities will come as no surprise when they arrive in the department. Academics have always considered collegiality to be a relevant criterion in hiring decisions (Bernard 1964; Harding 2002), even though university guidelines *say* that hiring and promotion should be based on academic merit. "Good colleagues" are usually defined as those with the necessary qualifications who also share similar intellectual interests, world views, social upbringing, behavioural norms, and even leisure pursuits (Bernard 1964; Brooks 1997; Jencks and Riesman 1977; Lamont 2009).

Although hiring usually involves committee decision making, it often becomes a major source of conflict because some faculty have more influence than others within the university or department. Each potential colleague could bring different qualities to the job, but faculty perceptions of strengths and weaknesses often vary by age, ethnicity, gender, and academic discipline, as well as rank and position. The local work culture also influences these perceptions. Especially in research universities, candidates from prestigious institutions who have international experience are sometimes viewed as more qualified and desirable than local applicants. This is particularly the case in jurisdictions where there are few qualified locals, such as Canada in the 1970s and New Zealand in more recent years.[1]

Acquiring the first tenure-stream job often involves relocating to find a position with an acceptable teaching load, opportunities for graduate supervision, and promotional prospects. Graduates lacking geographic mobility are forced to search locally for a job, but many communities have only one university. Even when there is more than one, no vacancies may exist in their field. Lack of mobility is often associated with family relationships, such as having a partner who cannot or will not relocate. Consequently, non-mobile graduates, who are typically women, sometimes accept part-time or temporary positions for years after graduation, often at the university where they received their PhD, in the hope that they will eventually be granted a permanent job. A few may eventually achieve this goal, but others are forced to seek non-academic positions or jobs in lower-status universities or colleges within commuting distance from home (Boreham et al. 2008; Mason, Goulden, and Wolfinger 2006; Valian 1998).

Hiring and Job Location: 1973

In the 1970s, anti-nepotism rules prevented many married women from being hired full-time at the university where their husband worked.

These rules assumed that hiring married couples would form an unfair and disruptive alliance within the department and that they would not be able to work together as ordinary colleagues. Of the thirty-nine women interviewed in the 1973 study, twenty-two were married, thirteen of them to academic men. Nine of the thirteen reported that anti-nepotism rules were used to deny them full-time jobs at the only university in the city, where their husband already worked (Baker 1975, 147).

One woman reported that after she was hired part-time in the 1960s, she had received a letter from the university president asking her to resign because he did not think that it was "proper" for her to be given a faculty position when her husband had a full-time appointment in another department. However, her departmental chairman fought to retain her. She claimed that she had worked long hours for seven years in a so-called part-time position without any employment benefits, but eventually she and her husband divorced. She then threatened to leave the university if it did not give her a full-time position with some job security and fringe benefits. At this point, she was offered a probationary position at the lowest rank (with no security), despite her seven years' experience, and was not offered a better position until she vehemently refused the initial offer (ibid., 152).

The interviewees were asked their opinions of anti-nepotism rules, which most viewed as unfair to women. A married assistant professor said, "I think they were concocted to disadvantage women," and a married associate professor made a similar comment: "They're rather foolish. A person's marital status should not be looked at ... It's nobody's business" (ibid., 148). Research also reports that nepotism rules typically work against women, as wives are usually younger than their husbands and often hold junior positions (Astin and Milem 1997; Creamer 2006). This marriage pattern remains prevalent today, as we will see in the next chapter.

Hiring and Job Location: 2008

Anti-nepotism rules now tend to be viewed as discriminatory, and many universities (including both the New Zealand ones) accept the idea of hiring academic couples, even in the same department. Furthermore, managers sometimes assist the partners of new hires to find employment within the university or community. However, scholars themselves do not always approve of having the spouse of a recently hired academic placed in their department by senior managers or of hiring couples in the same department if they might conspire regarding work-related decisions.

Despite the increased numbers of female academics, women are still most likely to work in teaching institutions or to be clustered in departments that place a high value on the pastoral care of students. They are typically expected to spend more hours per week in the classroom and to participate in more student-related meetings and events, and they may have to negotiate with their department head for designated research time. A female lecturer in the teaching university highlighted this pattern when she said, "The situation here is different from other universities – you have a higher teaching load. Research is very important to me ... so I have to maintain my research program and to negotiate that as well." According their students high priority reduces the opportunities of academics to specialize in their discipline, to design new research projects, and to publish peer-reviewed articles, which then influences their chances of promotion (Aisenberg and Harrington 1988; Bellas and Toutkoushian 1999; Leahey 2006; Middleton 2009).

Securing Tenure and Promotion

Gaining tenure or relative job security often implies a promotion to the next rank, although some universities require separate application processes for tenure and promotion. Regardless, achieving tenure and promotion involves assessment procedures based on similar academic criteria. In today's managerial environment, both typically necessitate complex application processes whereby faculty not only present their credentials but also provide written justifications and evidence of merit or excellence in teaching, research, and service.

For teaching, applications for tenure and promotion may include lists of undergraduate and graduate courses taught, graduate students supervised to completion, and student or peer teaching evaluations. For service or administration, applicants may be required to record the committees on which they served, the journals and granting agencies they assisted with peer reviewing, and other indicators of service to the university and profession. Promotion applications increasingly involve listing conference papers, publications, and research grants but also developing arguments about the worthiness or value of a candidate's scholarship in terms of peer evaluations and outcomes for stakeholders (Curtis and Matthewman 2005).

Applications typically include the promotion application itself, a curriculum vitae, samples of recent publications, and letters of recommendation. This dossier is then assessed by a committee of colleagues (that sometimes includes an equity officer), who make recommendations to university managers. For promotion to the highest ranks, recommendations from distinguished international professors are sometimes sought to verify the quality of the candidate's scholarship and international reputation. Senior promotions are often made centrally by university committees comprised of senior academics and managers, rather than by departmental or school committees.

Many studies find that promotion committees typically grant greater credibility to scholarship, research, and peer-reviewed publications than to teaching. This is especially the case in the research universities, where applicants must make strong arguments about the scholarly impact of their work (Burris 2004; Long 2001; Nakhaie 2007). Research is generally considered better if it is of international quality, meaning that it is published in books or journals that are scholarly, peer-reviewed, widely read by academics, and considered by other academics as prestigious (Lamont 2009). The ease with which academics gain promotion varies by discipline and department, but promotion requirements are more stringent at the most prominent universities.

If young academics have been well mentored and socialized into their disciplinary environment, they should understand the unwritten rules of the promotion process, but several women (though no men) in the New Zealand interviews did not seem to fully grasp the way that the system works. However, we need to acknowledge that receiving promotion can depend on factors outside the formal rules or an applicant's control, such as the composition of the promotion committee and members' personal opinions about the value of various types of productivity. The confidential letters of recommendation are also important for promotion. In some institutions, the university's ability to pay is alleged to be a factor in how many academics can be promoted in a particular year.

Especially in the research universities, women form a disproportionate percentage of part-time lecturers who are not required to engage in research or doctoral supervision, as well as junior academic staff with high loads of teaching preparation (Auriol 2007; Brooks 1997). Although gender differences are not always found in the number of courses taught or students supervised, studies have concluded that women spend more time than men on classroom preparation, teaching-related meetings, and student consultations (Fenton 2003; Joldersma 2005; Monroe et al. 2008).

Women often excel in teaching and administration, taking considerable pleasure from these roles, but these areas are commonly given a lower priority in promotion decisions (Brooks 1997; Nakhaie 2007). On average, women typically publish fewer refereed papers than men, largely because they work in disciplines and departments with a less developed research culture and a stronger emphasis on the pastoral care of students. However, as we will discuss in the next chapter, studies also show that more academic men than women enjoy domestic support at home (Leahey 2006; Xie and Shauman 1998).

In contrast, men have higher rates of application for externally funded research grants and more peer-reviewed publications (Fletcher et al. 2007; Leahey 2006). Consequently, more men are hired as prestigious research chairs, as I noted in Chapter 3 for the Canada Research Chair Program, but the percentage of male chairs is only slightly above the percentage of men in the higher ranks (Grant and Drakich 2010). Generally, male academics have longer careers, which contribute to reaching the top of the profession, because they are more likely than women to enter academia during or immediately after their doctorate. More women than men take career breaks for childrearing or enter the profession after having children or working in another occupation (Berberet et al. 2005; Jacobs 2004; Monroe et al. 2008; Tizard and Owen 2001).

Mobility and Work-Related Travel

Academics have always been a geographically mobile labour force, perhaps more than most other professional workers (Auriol 2010). Many leave their hometowns to complete doctorates in other places and re-locate again to find jobs or further promotions. Some seek positions in other countries. They also travel as part of their job, such as for confer-ences and sabbatical leave. In addition, some academics use geographical mobility to their advantage by applying for higher-ranking positions in other universities and securing job offers, using them as bargaining tools in their current job. These strategies were reported in earlier studies of the academic profession (Caplow and McGee 1958; Jencks and Riesman 1977) and persist today (Brooks and Mackinnon 2001; Lamont 2009). However, the academic job market has become more international, air travel is cheaper relative to wages, and travel arrangements can easily be made on the Internet.

In the 1970s, academic women in the liberal states had to contend with domicile laws that dictated that a wife's legal residence was wher-ever her husband lived (Backhouse 1991; Baker 2010b). If a wife sought employment and relocated to another town, she could be charged with desertion if her husband objected, and she could even lose custody of their children or her right to spousal support. Many participants in the 1973 study had come from the United States to seek work in the ex-panding Canadian university sector or to accompany their husband, who had been offered employment. Several who came with male part-ners complained that their husbands did not want them to work for pay, whereas anti-nepotism rules prevented others from finding full-time jobs at the only university in town. The study asked no further questions about work-related travel.

Many interviewees in the 2008 study came to New Zealand from other countries or were born there but had studied or worked overseas before returning. Most commented on the importance of family support for relocation, which is discussed more extensively in Chapter 5. How-ever, they often reported conference travel and sabbatical leave as con-tentious issues. Both men and women mentioned that the expense and sheer complication of taking the entire family overseas on research leave were becoming prohibitive but that if they went alone, they missed their children and partners.

A typical comment was made by a male lecturer with a young family who implied that sabbaticals with young children were costly and too complicated: "We are trying to figure out whether it makes sense to do an overseas sabbatical in the way that we have done previously, or whether it would make more sense to do a sabbatical and remain *here* so as to disrupt the children less."[2] With so many challenges relating to sabbaticals, some New Zealand-based academics went overseas for several short visits, which was more expensive than one longer trip but less disruptive to family life. Both universities encouraged and financially supported overseas travel during research leave because New Zealand is such a small island nation, far from much of the Western world. However, many scholars chose to remain in the country while on sabbatical leave and forfeit the university's travel grant.[3] All travel outside the country, even to Australia, requires at least a three-hour flight.

Participants in the 2008 study were asked whether they would consider looking elsewhere for a job if they were denied promotion at their current institution. Many of the men but few women answered positively. Several men also spoke of previous moves enabling them to gain higher rank and salaries, or of job offers that they used to negotiate with university managers for more resources or reduced teaching. Several interviewees also discussed the importance of relocation for promotion, mentioning that they had worked overseas and then returned to higher-ranking positions or came to New Zealand explicitly for promotional reasons.

In the 2008 interviews, men were far more likely than women to report both promotional opportunities at their current university and better job prospects in other countries. The women who said they would relocate for promotion tended to be single or childless, such as a female lecturer who felt that she would eventually have to leave New Zealand to get promoted to (full) professor because promotion was "too difficult" at the research university. She also commented that she needed work experience in another country for her area of specialization.

Men were much more likely than women to state that they had been contacted by a colleague or headhunter (personnel recruitment agency) to apply for a job in another country (usually Australia or the United Kingdom). In a few cases, senior-ranking men reported using this possibility or offer to negotiate for a better deal in their current job. For example, a man married to a successful businesswoman said, "Recently,

I've had two job offers from other places, and I have used those here to get better money and for extra leave. I got my leave extended from one semester to two. So, and in my experience it's the only time that the university will offer you anything ... I was offered a position at the University of [X] in Britain and I would have gone, but my wife didn't want to live in Britain."

Only two of the eighteen women in the study reported that they had been contacted by headhunters to apply for overseas jobs, but they did not see these opportunities as viable options and did not follow through. They assumed that their partner would be unable or unwilling to relocate, that their children's lives would be disrupted, or that they themselves would better off in their current job. None sent a curriculum vitae to the headhunter, went for an interview, or used the job prospect to negotiate with the dean for more resources. When I mentioned the option of using such offers as bargaining chips, several women expressed surprise that their colleagues employed this strategy. Most overtly disapproved of such tactics, whereas the men accepted them as normal practices. This suggests some differences in mentoring or integration into collegial networks between male and female academics.

Professional Integration

Bellas and Toutkoushian (1999) argue that (American) women publish less than men because they work more slowly and carefully due to heavier scrutiny of their research outputs and exclusion from collegial networks. These networks sometimes arise from casual interaction with colleagues sharing coffee or lunch breaks, often in same-sex groups. Most university departments contain more male than female academics, especially in senior ranks, which means that early-career men can more easily find same-sex colleagues to share breaks, discuss their work, gain mentoring, or become research collaborators (Bracken, Allen, and Dean 2006; Leahey 2006).

Academics in science, medicine, and engineering frequently work in research teams, where collegiality is essential. However, scholarship in the humanities and social sciences typically involves long hours of reading, searching for relevant material, and writing and rewriting articles, which can be isolating work even when it does entail team research and jointly authored publications. If scholars write alone, they may spend hours in their offices, not knowing whether colleagues will actually read the finished piece or accept their contribution to scholarship as worthwhile. Academic work could be even more isolating for women if there are few other women in the department, if they feel their research is undervalued by their male colleagues, or if they feel excluded from mainstream collegial networks.

Professional Integration: 1973

In the 1973 interviews, when few academic women worked full-time in university departments, there was considerable discussion among junior women about feeling marginal to collegial networks. They talked about gender discrimination from students and staff as well as sexual harassment. For example, an assistant professor from education mentioned that female academics are "given less respect and authority" and that students sometimes made "inappropriate sexual comments that aren't made about male professors" (Baker 1975, 128). She claimed that her male colleagues did not always perceive this as a form of discrimination unless it was pointed out to them.

A temporary lecturer in science talked about the "strong built-in prejudices" against academic women, especially among male students, and suggested that any "high voice, timidity or slight hesitancy on the part of a female lecturer encourages anti-woman feelings" (ibid., 175). A mature-age doctoral student married to a senior academic in the same department claimed that her professors viewed her as a "quaint oddity" and "talking dog" when she expressed interest in gaining a PhD. She claimed that she was treated either as a sex object or a threat and was assumed to have some sort of advantage due to her marital status. Because of her assumed lack of financial need, she was disqualified from any student assistantships and struggled to gain the necessary teaching and research experience for her desired academic career.

The participants also mentioned that some colleagues perceived female academics as less committed or as unprofessional, especially if they took employment leave for family reasons or left work early to supervise their school-aged children. If women were married, male colleagues assumed that they did not need their job or salary. An assistant professor reported that when she joined the department, she overheard one of her male colleagues saying, "What do we need a doctor's wife for?" suggesting that she did not need the job, because her husband was a professional. She stated that she was continually fighting the image of being the "doctor's wife" who was working just "to amuse [herself] or to make a point" (ibid., 135). A lecturer in the social sciences also mentioned that she heard colleagues making disparaging comments about "ladies dabbling in academia" (ibid., 156).

Several 1973 interviewees suggested that men gained peer esteem more easily than women and were therefore more readily promoted. For example, a full professor in the humanities said, "It is rare that a woman would be promoted without having better qualifications than a man" (ibid., 214). A woman in education made a similar comment: "There is more resistance to women in positions of authority and high prestige than at the junior levels" (ibid., 215). Twenty-five of the thirty-nine women reported examples of their gender interfering with promotion (ibid., 216). Yet they were divided about the value of affirmative action programs, with younger women more likely to support them.

A woman in science articulated academic women's powerlessness and susceptibility to exploitation in some of her comments: "Women have been work horses, and men have learned that if you have a job that you don't want to do yourself – give it to 'the girls'" (ibid., 145). A young married woman in the faculty of law also talked about the attitudes of her "conservative" colleagues: "Now that they know that I don't cry, I can take criticism, and that I can stand up to a class of ninety law students, I'm accepted as a colleague but I was on probation where a man wouldn't have been" (ibid., 157).

Women in the senior ranks were less likely to report exclusion from male networks or discrimination in academia. For instance, an associate professor in the social sciences mentioned that several "fuddy-duddies" in her department objected to being "out-published by a woman," but she claimed that these colleagues did not interfere in any way with her career. Another senior woman, the only woman in her department, offered this proviso: "Although I can talk confidentially with my colleagues and am not ostracized, there can be no group stance as I am the only woman" (ibid., 138).

Professional Integration: 2008

During the 2008 interviews, few women reported incidences of overt discrimination or sexual harassment, and more seemed to be integrated into collegial networks. However, several participants reported institutional experiences that diminished their motivation or made them feel unwelcome in academia. Most of these comments came from women, but two men also spoke about the negative work experiences of their academic wives. Two other men who prioritized teaching or came from working-class backgrounds hinted at feelings of marginalization in academia. However, many more women than men reported various forms of marginalization or disrespect.

Monroe and her colleagues (2008) argued that gender discrimination continues but has become more subtle over the years, partly through the process of gender devaluation where the power and status of an authoritative position is downplayed if it is held by a woman. There is some suggestion in other research that female managers in other types of work encounter more challenges to their authority than do male managers, especially if their management style goes against gender expectations (Acker 2010; Wolfram, Mohr, and Schyns 2007). A number of researchers have discussed the sidelining of women (and visible minorities), the chilly climate for academic women, and the unbreakable glass ceiling (Drakich et al. 1991; Kobayashi 2002; Side and Robbins 2007).

In many universities, academics are still comprised primarily of white males even when a growing portion of students and administrative staff are women and visible minorities. During the 2008 interviews, a participant from an ethnic minority background said, "Some of the people that I have to work with intimidate me and make me feel that I don't belong here." Clearly, academics and managers are not always aware that their behaviour or practices are perceived by others to be exclusionary.

Institutional Support for Gender Equity

Institutional support for gender equity has varied substantially over the decades and by institution and jurisdiction. In the 1973 study, the participants reported little support from the university or department, but few thought that the academic gender gap was caused or perpetuated by institutional priorities or practices. Instead, they maintained that it was the result of gender socialization or of raising girls to value relationships and families rather than careers. Senior women particularly felt that if more women were encouraged to continue their education, gain doctorates, and strive for professional positions, the academic gender gap would dissipate (Baker 1975, 141).

Participants in the 1973 study talked about being denied scholarships and permanent academic jobs because they were married women and of being perceived as unprofessional if they took time off for family reasons. Since then, paid parental leave and work-life balance programs have been developed, yet mothers continue to be penalized in the job market for parenthood and care activities (Correll, Benard, and Paik 2007; Gatta and Roos 2004; Glazer-Raymo 2008). In the 2008 interviews, mothers told disheartening stories of juggling parental leave with their teaching requirements and organizing breastfeeding between classes. They also talked about squiring children to and from day care, searching for emergency care for sick children, and dealing with childcare problems during research and conference leave. Most of the mothers reported little support for these challenges from university managers, unions, or colleagues.

The mothers in both studies commented that managers and colleagues found it difficult to accommodate maternity leave even when it was part of the collective agreement. In the 2008 interviews, a junior-ranking mother from the research university provided an example of the lack of institutional support when she said, "There was another young woman who had a child very shortly after me. So it was sort of a double whammy for the department, and I think they found that a bit difficult to deal with ... They didn't really know how to handle this ... Somebody actually said to me when I was on [maternity] leave, 'Oh you'll have so much time to do all this work.' And I'm, like, 'Well, I'll have a newborn baby! I won't have any time at all!' There's certainly a set of expectations that being on maternity leave is somehow a kind of holiday [*laughter*]."

Another single mother from the research university said, "When I first came back to work [from maternity leave], I was scheduled to teach from 5:00 p.m. until 6:00 p.m. three days a week and the [university] crèche closes at 5:00. And so there were just kinds of simple practical things like that that I had to sort of go and say, 'Look, this isn't workable, this isn't feasible, I can't do this,' and there was just not really the kinds of systems set up, you know?" An older mother, now in a senior position in the research university, spoke of past difficulties when she had a baby over a decade ago: "I had a fairly strict head of department who made it very clear that there were going to be no concessions allowed. So that was very demanding – being responsible for a new baby, breastfeeding and all that ... That first year with my first child was difficult. I did manage to carry on ... Yeah, one does, I suppose."

Despite recent improvements to parental leave policies, both men and women in the 2008 study agreed that parenthood still made a huge impact on women's careers. Consequently, a disproportionate number of female participants felt that combining childbearing with an academic career was too challenging and made comments such as, "I only had one [child] because it was far too hard." A childless woman in her late thirties said, "I work very, very hard, in a way that I never could if I had kids. I hear stories about the struggles of my colleagues who are mothers." These issues will be discussed in more detail in Chapter 5.

Work organizations are often insensitive to family-related problems because they have competing strategic goals, such as balancing their budgets, meeting government requirements, or ensuring that students complete their degrees. In the 2008 interviews, a senior academic who was a married father noted that families tend to be invisible in academia, which is a problem for *all* parents: "I think one of the things I found interesting about working in universities is not that they're gender blind, it's that they're family blind. The two go together, of course, but I'm really quite struck and often quite shocked by how invisible family is in a work setting."

Responding to the Changing Work Culture

Enhancing the Focus on Research and Internationalization

In the current university environment, promotional decisions not only favour research over teaching but also create a hierarchy of research methodologies and publication venues (Burris 2004; Harding 2002). Although these preferences are not usually stipulated in promotion guidelines, they informally influence decision making in many universities (Harley 2003; Lucas 2006; Reimer 2004). These priorities are further strengthened by national and international ranking systems (Thomas and Davies 2002).

Some disciplines and departments place heightened pressure on academics to publish in scholarly journals with high impact ratings, as these are widely read by academics and are considered more competitive and prestigious. Publishing textbooks, edited books, or articles in less prominent journals is usually considered to be of less importance. Greater value is also given to projects supported by competitive research grants, which often reduce university costs. Projects that involve collaborative partners from other institutions and those using quantitative methodologies are also favoured. However, several studies have found that women's research projects tend to differ from men's. For example, they are more often smaller in scale, applied and based on local research, and reliant on qualitative research, feminist theories, and female subjects and collaborators (Knights and Richards 2003; Leahey 2006; Long 2001; Wyn, Acker, and Richards 2000).

In the 2008 interviews, the recently hired subjects expected to spend a substantial portion of their time on research.[4] One interview question was, "What aspects of academic work do you enjoy most?" Participants from the research university typically focused on research. For instance, a female lecturer answered, "I guess I prioritize my research, and anything that disrupts my research, I don't like, quite frankly." Another female lecturer at the research university said, "This is a space where I can marry my passion with my career ... As long as I make article deadlines and work on books, then my space here is secured." At the teaching university, recently hired and younger participants also valued their research time and saw few problems with increased productivity pressures. For example, a male senior lecturer talked about research as the best part of the job: "The research – it's nice to have a journal article that comes back and they say yes. It gives me a glowing feeling ... I hope I never publish that much that the feeling goes away." A female senior lecturer from the same university said, "I don't mind working really hard for the research projects. I do mind working really hard if ... too much of that time is taken up with admin."

The stronger emphasis on research was particularly difficult for those at the teaching university who had neither a PhD nor much research experience but who had a high teaching load, or who had to negotiate research time in a department with a strong teaching culture. The following comment from a female lecturer at the teaching university highlights the differences between the two types of university: "This is a teaching institution and the place of teaching is marked out very strongly, and there are only about six of us within this department of eighty people who are research-active and with PhDs."

The priority granted to internationalization also works disproportionately against academics with local backgrounds, lower salaries, and young children. All three categories include more women than men. International collaboration requires wide academic networks, often gained from working internationally, but women are less likely than men to make international career moves that expand their networks. Work-related travel is made easier by external research grants that include travel funds, or at least by receiving more travel funds than are normally allocated by university departments. Academics in senior positions (mainly male) are most likely to receive large external research grants, but men also have higher application rates for external grants (Waisbren et al. 2008). In addition, they have higher average salaries than women in academia and fewer responsibilities for the daily care of children.

Administrative Changes and Managerialism

In the 2008 interviews, several participants from the teaching university commented that it was changing too fast, had a high turnover of managers, placed unreasonable workload expectations on staff, and was promoting "outsiders" more quickly than long-term local staff. For instance, a woman senior lecturer seemed very distressed by recent changes: "Staff are exploited here. Teaching loads are too high!" Another woman from the same institution and the same rank said that the university "is very hierarchical and bureaucratic, but they keep appointing people ... They've got vice chancellor and pro vice chancellors and deans and heads of school and, oh, heads of department, program leaders ... And really, you feel like you're on the shop floor, and you've got all these managers telling you what to do." She added, "I have been here thirteen years, and I've had eleven heads of school. I have prepared about 250 different lectures because my teaching keeps getting changed ... I'm often stressed but I am never bored [*laughter*]."

Participants from both universities mentioned that their love of scholarship was being destroyed by increasing levels of bureaucracy and reporting requirements. A senior woman who was about to retire from the research university said, "I have mostly always loved my job, though in the last twenty years I think that things have become steadily more unpleasant for academics actually. It is not the wonderful job that it used to be ... I think there's just such a wealth of bureaucracy, and there's so much monitoring and inventing justifications and descriptions of what one is doing that to me have no real relationship to which I'm doing [*laughter*] ... Under that heading, I'm including filling in PBRF forms."

Academic men made similar comments, including a senior man who lamented the additional reporting requirements for department heads at the research university: "I must say I find the increasing administration and the increasing requirements and requests from academic staff, but the lack of delegation of authority to do them, frustrating. So I now have to produce an enormous amount of paperwork and sign things, but then someone else further up the chain won't accept the signature!" Both men and women voiced these complaints, but older women from the teaching university seemed especially concerned about the negative impact of institutional restructuring on their job satisfaction and promotion prospects. Younger academics who had recently entered the profession were more likely to see these requirements as normal.

Participants from both universities remarked on the competitive academic environment, the demise of collegiality, and the rise of managerialism. A female interviewee who had taught part-time at the research university mentioned that she moved to the teaching university to gain a permanent position. Like the wider research, she suggested that both types of university have become more managerial: "I missed a lot of what was going on [at the research university] and the collegiality and the focus on academic stuff rather than the sort of bureaucratic things here. But unfortunately, what's happened is everything's got more bureaucratic and managerial, and [the research university] now is not the same place at all."

Long-Hours Culture

The long-hours culture is widespread in universities, with many academics reporting that they are working harder and longer than in the past without necessarily getting ahead (Kinman and Jones 2004; Menzies and Newson 2008). In my 2008 interviews, both men and women commented on the long hours required to retain their jobs and achieve promotion. For example, a senior man, who was also a father married to another academic, said, "What would be hard for a lot of people is the fact that the research questions never go away, or the next book project is always on your mind, which is very different from a lot of professions out there." Some found the all-encompassing nature of the job challenging, and several openly acknowledged that they worked every weekend and saw themselves as "workaholics." A senior woman from the research university suggested that academics actually need to be "workaholics," "compulsive personalities," and "obsessive" if they wish to get ahead in the profession.

The female interviewees tended to object more than the men to the lengthy working hours. For instance, a woman senior lecturer from the teaching university said, "I find myself working over weekends to live up to expectations that have been set on us." A female professor on the cusp of retiring from the research university justified her decision to leave paid work by saying, "I started to get a bit stressed about the way in which I was working right through every weekend as well as often quite late at night ... I just thought that I'd quite like my life back now for myself, to do things that I enjoy doing." The long-hours work culture and heightened requirements of productivity are particularly challenging for older workers and mothers with young children, especially single mothers.

Several studies suggest that long hours are viewed differently depending on who works them: putting in long hours is sometimes seen as a choice for women but a requirement for men (Bernard 1988; Probert 2005; White 2004; Wilson, Gadbois, and Nichol 2008). Partnered women are still less likely to be perceived as the main household earner, but more women also report that they value a balanced life over career success, which will be discussed in Chapter 6.

Conclusion

Locating effective mentors and role models, finding the best university job, focusing on research and publishing, working long hours, and remaining employed for many years without interruption are all important for research productivity, peer esteem, and promotion to the highest ranks of academia. However, these aspects of academic and social capital are influenced by access to support and material circumstances, which tend to vary by gender.

Since the 1970s, more women have been employed as university academics and more have been promoted to senior positions. This change in the gender balance has been accompanied by a degree of continuity in academic priorities and standards, as well as the social capital that men and women bring to their careers. The two sets of interview data presented in this chapter – gathered more than thirty years apart and in different countries – show that many of the institutional and collegial concerns of 1973 continue in the twenty-first century. Researchers have also found the persistence of gendered relations in other work organizations in the liberal states (Alvesson and Billing 2009; Pettit and Hook 2009; Sax 2008).

More women are pursuing doctorates and academic jobs, but more women than men "leak out of the pipeline" prior to attaining permanent university positions (CAUT 2011b; Mason, Goulden, and Wolfinger 2006). Academic careers are still influenced by gendered access to mentoring, research sponsors, and collegial networks, and by the availability of positive role models. Many women enter tenure-stream jobs later than men, particularly after raising children or working in another occupation, and they tend to retire earlier after shorter careers. When scholars enter their profession at the same age and work full-time throughout their lives, they increase their chances of reaching the professoriate. More women may fill the new vacancies as senior men retire, although some permanent positions will inevitably be lost as universities continue to restructure (Acker 2003; Curtis and Matthewman 2005).

Public universities are now focusing more on their research capacities and capabilities, attempting to increase their national and international status. This tendency has reinforced the advantage of academics with high qualifications and those who single-mindedly pursue their research interests, develop collegial networks, author publications, and increase their peer esteem. Most participants in the 2008 study discussed the heightened expectations of research productivity at their university, as well as the higher student enrolments, greater levels of management, and increased pressure to perform their job in certain ways. Most believed that they worked very hard and deserved (but did not always receive) more institutional and collegial recognition for their efforts. However, the male subjects seemed more knowledgeable about university practices and more accepting of the competitive and long-hours culture.

Since the 1970s, universities have taken equity issues more seriously, but vast differences exist by jurisdiction, institution, and department. Despite developing formal programs for equity hiring, mentoring, and parental and family-related leave, universities have been unable to create a level playing field for men and women. The age-old disciplinary priorities and practices, and the new political and economic pressures, continue alongside institutional concerns about equity and sometimes serve to diminish them. The most significant criteria for promotion to the senior ranks in many universities continue to be high-impact research outcomes rather than teaching skills or departmental service. In addition, the corporatized university tends to favour masculinized behaviour that is competitive, individualistic, and often confrontational, which many women feel uncomfortable with (Fletcher et al. 2007).

Acknowledging gender differences clearly involves challenges for both managers and colleagues, such as finding teaching replacements during maternity/parental leave and mentoring women without paternalism or favouritism. Nonetheless, universities could do more to improve women's academic status. Women's research could more often be showcased in the academy and professional associations, and male colleagues could be encouraged by department heads to take it more seriously. Managers could also attempt to find a more equitable gender balance in teaching and service positions, encouraging men to devote more time to student activities and committee work.

Gendered Families and the Motherhood Penalty

5

If a woman is not married, they assume that she is either a recluse or will run off and get married any minute. If she is married, then they assume her family responsibilities will interfere with her job.

– FEMALE DOCTORAL STUDENT, CANADA, 1973

I know parenting is both of our responsibilities ... but as the mother realistically I feel the pull more than he does to be at home and be the main nurturer in our family.

– FEMALE LECTURER, NEW ZEALAND, 2008

Parental Support for Doctorate and Career

Studies have found that parental encouragement and especially the social class background of one's family continue to shape educational choices and achievement levels (Reay at al. 2001; Van De Werfhorst, Sullivan, and Cheung 2003). Parents who earned university degrees or who value tertiary education and occupational success will generally encourage their children to excel in school, continue their education to university graduation, and aspire to professional or managerial careers. In addition, young people with family financial support or scholarships have more opportunities to pursue their studies to the highest level, to attend the best universities, and to progress through the ranks of their chosen profession.

Parental Support: 1973

In the Canadian study, many of the participants reported that they had been encouraged by parents and/or teachers to continue their education at a time when only about 10 percent of new doctorates were awarded to women. This suggests that these women were already contravening gendered practices by gaining a PhD, but many also came from privileged families that emphasized the importance of postsecondary education. For example, an associate professor of education from a wealthy American family mentioned, "In my family, it was not a matter of *were* you going to college but *where* were you going to college" (Baker 1975, 164). However, in the 1970s, less parental or societal support was available for these women to pursue full-time professional careers.

A lecturer in education stated that her mother encouraged her to attend university – even to study law – but never thought that she would finish her degree or work as a lawyer. Neither of her parents thought that she would take her studies seriously "but saw a career as *insurance* in case I did not get married, or as something to do before marriage" (ibid., 167). In a similar vein, another woman in law mentioned that her father was concerned that she would become "too hard-nosed" and would "move too far away from my *natural* role as wife and mother" (ibid., 166). In some instances, parents were quite unsupportive. For example, an associate professor in education reported that her father had never acknowledged that she had received a doctorate and had never congratulated her. These comments suggest that middle-class parents may have encouraged their daughters to obtain a postsecondary education in the 1960s and '70s but did not always expect them to pursue a professional or male-dominated career. Instead, they typically anticipated that they would become wives and mothers.

Parental Support: 2008

Nearly half of recent doctorates are now awarded to women, suitable academic role models are available for them, and it is more acceptable to live outside marriage. This means that fewer unmarried career women would be viewed by others or would see themselves as atypical or deviant. However, having supportive parents still makes it easier for both sexes to develop successful and satisfying careers. In the 2008 interviews, several participants from the research university mentioned that their parents had tertiary degrees, were academics or other high-level professionals, or were "self-taught intellectuals" who encouraged them to strive for academic excellence. For example, one young male lecturer who had recently come to the research university from a privileged North American family talked about his decision to get his doctorate: "It's always been in the back of my mind. My dad has a double doctorate, he's got a PhD and a DDS, and my mother's an MD. So it was just kind of ... it was a natural thing to do. I've always been reasonably good at education, so it was just natural progression. It was kind of the next thing to do."

Many interviewees talked about their father's influence on their decision to pursue and complete a doctorate. For instance, a (full) professor, who was a married father, said, "My dad was fantastic ... genuinely interested in my PhD. He used to read my draft chapters and talk to me about them." A senior woman, who was unmarried without children, also reported strong paternal support for her doctorate: "I come from an academic background, so I've kind of taken in a certain amount of knowledge from my father ... So I guess I always thought that I had a bit of a headstart in that sense of having that kind of knowledge." Paternal encouragement seemed to be important for both male and female participants.

We tend to think that indifferent or unsupportive parents will produce children who are low achievers, but not all subjects in the 2008 study reported that their parents encouraged them to pursue an academic career, especially among the older women. Several spoke of their parents' distinct lack of interest in their doctorate and academic career, even though some of them had already reached the senior professoriate. For instance, a senior woman who was also a mother said, "My mother definitely was a bit discouraging [about me doing a doctorate], couldn't understand why I bothered. My father was proud ... but fairly non-committal." Another senior professor (also a mother) said, "My father died when I was young, and my mother thought I should get married. She didn't disapprove [of me doing a doctorate] but didn't encourage it." Several participants who reported little family support nevertheless reached the highest academic rank – through "sheer hard work," as the previous woman put it. However, they implied that their career decisions were more attributable to academic mentors than to parents.

Others seemed to experience multiple family obstacles, such as lack of parental support or additional family/cultural responsibilities. A female senior lecturer from the teaching university said, "My family could never work out why I ever went to university, and so I had no family support for this direction at all ... I come from a working-class background." A woman lecturer at the research university, who also came from a working-class family, spoke of her mother's lack of education and a cultural background that did not encourage the pursuit of an "individualistic career." Participants who mentioned lack of parental support were more often women, those from working-class backgrounds, and those with few expectations of reaching the highest academic rank. Furthermore, a number of women actually talked about their home-maker mothers as *negative* role models, such as this female senior lecturer who said, "I saw my own mother who was stuck in a very traditional gender role, and I never wanted to have a life like that!"

Participants also mentioned parental support with caring work, which particularly enabled the mothers to pursue their career while raising young children. For example, one single mother said, "My parents both work but they generally come once a week and pick [my child] up and take him home so I can work late." A partnered mother said, "We both have family here, and they do babysitting and things like that." Most who talked about this kind of parental support with physical parenting were women, and those who mentioned it seemed more optimistic about their ability to handle the integration of their academic career and family care work.

This kind of parental assistance, however, sometimes came with strings attached or was no longer feasible for reasons of geographic distance or aging parents. For instance, a male participant reported that his mother-in-law interfered with his domestic affairs and criticized his wife's career aspirations, housekeeping, and childrearing practices when she came to their home to care for her grandchildren while both parents worked. Partly for this reason, his wife eventually accepted a job in another New Zealand city, relocating the children there, which required him to face a long-distance commute to work.

Many academics in the 2008 study were migrants from other countries or regions and therefore had no daily or physical family support. For example, a single mother from the research university said that the sheer distance from the rest of her family in the United States meant that relying on their assistance was too complicated: "I don't have any family members in New Zealand, so there's not somebody I can turn to, like a mother or a sister ... In the past, I've left [my daughter] with my mother or my sister for archival trips and the same with conferences. I went to one conference in Bangkok, and that involved me flying from Auckland to Los Angeles to [a US state] to drop [the child] off, to then go back across to Bangkok and go back to pick her up, and, you know, I was exhausted by the end of it ... Now I need to go to Wellington [in New Zealand] to look at some material for the book that I'm writing ... but I'll wait until my mom is coming." However, her mother was in her eighties, which meant that this kind of practical childcare support was unsustainable but also unaffordable, as it involved considerable travel and extra expense for both women.

In both sets of interviews, parents and other family members were seen as sources of support but also as obstacles to overcome when participants discussed completing their doctorates and establishing academic careers. However, many stated that support from a partner was more consequential for their career development.

Marriage and Partner Support

Studying the personal lives of academics allows us to identify patterns of intimate relationships that could contribute to the gender gap, and previous research has found similar trends within all the liberal states. First, studies have shown that academic men are more likely than their female counterparts to be married and to have more children, whereas academic women are more likely to be single, separated, divorced, and single parents (Bellas 1994; Brooks 1997; Toutkoushian, Bellas, and Moore 2007; Wolfinger, Mason, and Goulden 2008). Earlier research on New

Zealand academics found that about 85 percent of men and 56 percent of women were married, 6 percent of men and 19 percent of women were separated or divorced, and 8 percent of men and 24 percent of women had never married (Brooks 1997, 74). More recent figures from the United States show that twelve years after receiving their doctorate, 69 percent of men in tenured or tenure-track positions were married with children, compared to only 41 percent of women (Mason, Goulden, and Wolfinger 2006). Despite minor variations by jurisdiction and specific study, these broad family patterns remain similar throughout the liberal states.

Second, a marriage gradient often occurs in the general population, with men marrying "down" in terms of age, educational attainment, and occupational status (Baker 2010b). Academics tend to follow this pattern as well. For example, Mason, Goulden, and Wolfinger (2006) found that married male doctoral students in the United States were more likely than their female counterparts to have younger partners with part-time, temporary, or no paid jobs. Marriage to a "junior" partner enables a couple to view the husband's career as more important but also permits him to relocate more easily and to devote longer hours to his scholarly work with fewer effective objections from his wife (Bracken, Allen, and Dean 2006; McMahon 1999). Especially when work environments require increased productivity and more international travel, promotion can be enhanced by having a supportive partner, particularly if he or she accords priority to the partner's career and is willing to shoulder much of the domestic work.

Third, academic women with partners are more likely than partnered academic men to be in dual-career marriages, especially those in which both spouses work more than forty hours a week (O'Laughlin and Bischoff 2005). Jacobs (2004) found that 89 percent of female academics but only 56 percent of male academics in the United States had partners who were employed full-time. Academic women are also more likely to partner with another academic, especially in second or subsequent marriages (Astin and Milem 1997; Creamer 2006). Among partnered academics in Astin and Milem's (1997) American study, 40 percent of women and 35 percent of men reported having spouses or partners who also worked in postsecondary education. Working in the same occupation and especially at the same university could provide more partner support for one's career (Ferber and Loeb 1997). For example, a woman lecturer in the 2008 interviews commented, "If your partner is also in the same institution ... you don't have to be explaining your long work hours, you don't have to explain the weirdness of being an academic, because the other person understands." However, this also suggests that female academics are more likely to have partners who work long hours and cannot share the household chores.

Marriage or a stable cohabiting relationship is often considered to be an asset for promotion in professional jobs because each tends to represent a form of maturity and social integration in the eyes of colleagues (Toutkoushian, Bellas, and Moore 2007). Research suggests that marriage to a non-employed spouse is a definite asset for men's academic salary and promotion (Bellas 1994), whereas marriage to a professional man is an asset for women's initial promotion but not for subsequent ones (Long and Fox 1995). Xie and Shauman (1998) concluded that both male and female scholars benefit from the human capital of having a highly educated spouse, which tends to enhance their academic networks and research productivity. Perhaps one could argue that this is actually a form of *social* capital.

Academic couples often read and critique each other's papers and sometimes publish together. However, male partners tend to have a higher rank and salary, and are reported to work longer hours for pay than female partners (M. Fox 2005; O'Laughlin and Bischoff 2005). Several North American studies suggest that women married to male scholars need to maintain some intellectual autonomy from their partner early in their careers in order to gain promotion (Creamer 2006; Ferber and Loeb 1997; Loeb 2001; Wolf-Wendel, Twombly, and Rice 2003). Otherwise, their husband (and other male collaborators) tend to be given a disproportionate amount of credit for any joint publications (Nakhaie 2007; Rossiter 1993).

Partner Support: 1973

In my Canadian study, a substantial number of female doctoral students and academics were unmarried or divorced at a time when general marriage rates were historically high, the age of marriage had reached a low point in that century, unmarried cohabitation was rare, and divorce laws were restrictive in all the countries under study (although they were more flexible in several American states) (Baker 2010b; Beaujot 2000). Consequently, remaining single was unusual at the time, although it was more prevalent for academic women. One unmarried doctoral student in education commented, "I am a bit of an embarrassment to my parents, as [my] mother thinks that being unmarried is unnatural and sad" (Baker 1975, 183). Another unmarried doctoral student in the social sciences stated, "I am aware of the pressures to marry and aware that I am bucking the stereotype. The biggest hurdle for a single woman to overcome is social ostracism." Later she talked about the "double bind" that applies to women: "If a woman is not married, they assume that she is either a recluse or will run off and get married any minute. If she is married, then they assume her family responsibilities will interfere with her job" (ibid., 183).

Several married women in the 1973 study talked about supportive husbands who strongly encouraged them to complete their PhDs and pursue an academic career. For instance, an associate professor of education spoke about her husband's support, stating that he had "no desire for the kind of wife who stays at home and diddles around the house" (ibid., 168). However, not all the interviewees were fortunate enough to have supportive husbands. One temporary lecturer in the humanities said that her former husband "generally disapproved of women working outside the home" (ibid., 169). The couple eventually divorced and she returned to university to complete her PhD.

The 1973 interviews showed a trend in which women who reported a lack of career support from their partner experienced more work/family conflict and had a lower academic rank. However, several rationalized their temporary appointments and low salaries by stating that they were "grateful for the appointment." This was especially the case for married women who had difficulty finding work at the same university as their husband, due to anti-nepotism rules. After a period of unemployment, some accepted any job offer, asking few questions about the salary and without attempting to bargain for anything better (ibid., 135).

Partner Support: 2008

In the New Zealand study, in which participants were chosen largely by rank, more men than women were married or in long-term relationships with younger partners, and more were parents. All of the twelve men (100 percent) were married or cohabiting, and eight (67 percent) were fathers, with another two young men contemplating fatherhood in the near future. In contrast, ten of the eighteen women (56 percent) were married or cohabiting (some with substantially older men and one with a woman). Only ten (56 percent) were mothers, and five of these were single parents. Among the partnered subjects, three women said that their male partners were retired or semi-retired, but a higher percentage of men reported partners who did not have paid work. Most of the men mentioned that their partners had worked part-time at some stage in their lives, had changed occupations, and/or reduced their employment hours with his career moves. As Table 5.1 indicates, fewer women than men were married and were parents, and fewer women at the higher ranks were mothers than were women at the lower ranks. Both aspects of my sample are consistent with overseas research.

Research on the academic gender gap generally reveals that most married academics, including women, report that their partner supported their career (O'Laughlin and Bischoff 2005). The 2008 interviews showed similar findings. Most of the married or cohabiting participants

Table 5.1 Marital and parental status of 2008 participants (number of participants)

Rank	Male		Female	
	Married or cohabiting	*Father*	*Married or cohabiting*	*Mother*
Lecturer or senior lecturer	7/7	4/7	6/12	8/12
Associate prof or professor	5/5	4/5	4/6	2/6
Total	12/12	8/12	10/18	10/18
Percent	100	67	56	56

mentioned supportive partners, such as this young mother with a self-employed husband, who said, "I've been very lucky to have somebody who is incredibly supportive ... I don't think I would have been able to do all kinds of things that I have done if I hadn't had somebody who was ... there with me all the way through it."

A senior woman on the cusp of retirement also said, "It's certainly been terribly important to me to have a partner who was also an academic and was understanding and supportive." Her cohabiting partner of many decades had worked in the same department but took early retirement before she did and at a lower rank than she held. A male senior lecturer at the teaching university also spoke at length about his supportive partner, who was an academic at another university in the same city: "She has academic skills that complement mine, and she helps me out in my own work sometimes. If I've got a journal article that I'm writing, I can hand it to her and she can go through it and proofread it and say, 'Not sure whether you've covered this enough.'"

Participants also told stories about unsupportive spouses, although most of these were ex-partners at the time of the interview. One male professor related an anecdote about his first wife, who would not allow him to discuss work-related matters at home and failed to take any interest in his first book, although he added that she was willing to give dinner parties for his visiting colleagues. He later mentioned that his current wife is much more supportive and accommodating. In contrast, a number of women reported making major career sacrifices for ex-husbands who failed to acknowledge or appreciate their support. For example, a senior professor in her sixties spoke about moving with her first husband, shortly after she completed her doctorate on scholarship in Europe: "I went [to North America] as a visiting scholar's wife, and ... eventually I found a job ... He went because he was looking for more challenges." When asked "Were you also looking for more challenges?" she replied, "Not at that point but I went along with it." This woman talked about life with her husband when she was a young academic living in North America: "His career came first ... to both of us ... Essentially, all the childcare was my responsibility." She returned to New Zealand when the marriage was clearly over and later remarried, retaining a gendered division of labour in her second marriage. Previous studies report that separation/divorce is widespread during the doctorate and early career, especially for women (Brooks 1997; O'Laughlin and Bischoff 2005). However, few academic women working full-time would now accept such a gendered division of labour as this senior professor in the New Zealand study, suggesting a generational change.

Several women in the 2008 study commented on the fact that they had no partner with whom they could share their career triumphs and tribulations, or the domestic workload, which was both an advantage and a disadvantage. A senior academic, who was single and child-free, expressed this very plainly:

> It's *clearly* an advantage being single, instead of trying to carry the double load that a lot of my women friends do. But it has its down side because, of course, if you are single you end up doing all the chores yourself. In terms of support ... people with partners take for granted that when they go home there is someone there to moan to [small ironic laugh] if need be, or celebrate things with. So, yeah, there's obviously some pluses and minuses to being single and working fairly intensively ... It's very easy to neglect having a social life ... When I look at my colleagues that do have families, they're forced to take time for that. So, it's both a burden but also sustenance. So [my] life's simpler ... but in some ways tougher.

A young single mother, who had recently arrived from overseas, expressed a typical female concern about lack of support at home: "Men seem to have no problems setting roots as young academics because they have women to look after them. I needed a wife, if that makes sense ... I mean, for me, it's a high-pressure kind of job and to be in a foreign country." In these interviews, marriage seemed to be a form of social capital for many men but for fewer women. In fact, some subjects noted that marriage could negatively alter colleagues' perceptions about young women's commitment to the job. As one young unmarried female lecturer said, "Guys might say that when they apply for a job being married is seen as a good thing, that they're seen as 'long-term.' I don't know if that's the same for women, that you might be seen to be a bit risky if you're married because then you might want to have children."

Both sets of interviews included participants who reported that the female partner began her career with higher academic qualifications than her husband or was the first to receive a doctorate or academic position. At the time of the interview, however, the male partner held a more senior job or was working full-time, whereas the woman had downsized to part-time work or changed careers, usually to one of lower prestige. These examples reflect a wider pattern, prevalent in the past but continuing today, of couples giving priority to the man's career or women withdrawing from the job market for childrearing. However, when childrearing is completed, these mothers seldom catch up to their male colleagues or partner in terms of salary and promotion.

Having and Raising Children
Parenthood and living with young children are generally associated with employment and earnings advantages for men but with disadvantages for women (Correll, Benard, and Paik 2007; Zhang 2009). More women than men academics report that they are the primary caregiver of young children or have caring responsibilities for other relatives, and researchers typically conclude that "babies matter" to women's academic promotion (Comer and Stites-Doe 2006; Ferber and Loeb 1997; M. Fox 2005; Grummell, Devine, and Lynch 2009; Mason, Goulden, and Wolfinger 2006; O'Laughlin and Bischoff 2005). That said, female academics are more likely than other high-achieving career women to remain childless, whereas male academics are more likely than other male professionals to become fathers (Bassett 2005; Hewlett and Vite León 2002).

Studies from several liberal states have noted that childlessness is more prevalent among tenure-track and tenured academic women, whereas a higher percentage of non-tenure-track women are married mothers working part-time (Brooks 1997; Harper et al. 2001; Mason and Goulden 2002, 2004). Among tenure-track academics, more women than men are also single or divorced, and academic women are much more likely than academic men to become single parents (M. Fox 2005; Mason, Goulden, and Wolfinger 2006; Moyer, Salovey, and Casey-Cannon 1999;

O'Laughlin and Bischoff 2005). Finally, mothers are less likely than fathers or childless women to reach the senior ranks of academia (Monroe et al. 2008; Probert 2005), which effectively illustrates the motherhood penalty.

Most academics have their children at the start of their career, before they achieve job security. American studies find that academic women who have babies within five years of earning a doctorate are less likely than childless women or academic men to receive tenure or job security (Mason and Goulden 2002). Female PhDs who are outside the labour force tend to have the highest fertility rate, followed by part-time women academics, and then full-time women in tenure-stream positions. This suggests that women who enter full-time tenure-track positions are either less interested in motherhood or find combining it with a full-time academic career to be too difficult.

Studies of academic work find that pregnancy and infant care particularly interfere with women's search for the first tenure-stream job, as well as with subsequent research and publishing (Bassett 2005; Bracken, Allen, and Dean 2006; Mason, Goulden, and Wolfinger 2006). Women doctorates who are pregnant or who have young children are less likely than other women or men doctorates to find a full-time academic job immediately after graduation. They are also more likely to manage their work-life balance through part-time or temporary positions early in their career. Some continue to opt out of the labour force when their children are young, although fewer now choose this route. Women doctorates with children and full-time tenure-track positions may have found satisfactory childcare services and/or domestic support from their partners or other family members (Valian 1998).

On average, academic women publish less than academic men, but not all studies find that parents publish less than non-parents. Wolf-Wendel, Twombly, and Rice (2003) report that married academics tend to be more productive than single ones, although more men than women are married. Mary Fox (2005) found that American women with school-aged children publish more than other academic women, which may reflect a generational difference in work practices or their self-selection as determined workers with high levels of personal efficiency. However, the impact of children on women's careers has certainly changed over the decades.

Children and Academic Careers: 1973

Many women in the Canadian study reported traditional households with a gendered division of labour. Most married women and mothers stated that they had to work harder than men to incorporate both their academic work and domestic duties. One woman said, "Society is set up in such a way to give women a double load. The more conscientious they are about bringing up their families, the more they are penalized" (Baker 1975, 180). An assistant professor stated that she had to work "one-and-a-half to two times as hard as a man to keep everything going ... My husband has a traditional view of women and doesn't help out at home (ibid., 177). In addition, several mothers said that their attention was "divided" between university work and childcare; some interviewees saw this as a reason to avoid motherhood. For example, a childless associate professor in education commented, "Teaching university is a very full-time job. If I had children, something would get lost in the shuffle. Can you really have both and do it well?" (ibid., 178). In this study, the mothers who maintained a traditional division of labour at home generally held a lower rank and often a part-time or temporary job.

Some of the mothers in the 1973 study deliberately requested part-time work so as to focus on family care, but some mistakenly expected that they would be able to secure a permanent academic position when they were ready to take on more responsibility. Others managed to move to tenure-stream jobs. For example, a full professor mentioned that she had initially been given a temporary appointment even though she had a PhD; she also made one-third of the salary her husband received without a doctorate. However, she quickly added, "I wanted a part-time job until I was sure that I could handle a full-time job and my baby." Despite the fact that she worked the equivalent of full-time hours, she stated that her salary "seemed reasonable at the time" and would not refer to her situation as sex discrimination (ibid., 136). By current standards, and in light of recent policies to make workplaces more sympathetic to parents, some of these interview comments sound very sexist and antiquated.

Children and Academic Careers: 2008

Compared to those of the 1973 study, more 2008 participants cohabited without legal marriage, but they typically postponed parenthood until they obtained a doctorate and found a permanent university job. Most interviewees saw having children as desirable, but the women were more likely to view them as career obstacles. At the time, several participants were weighing the advantages and disadvantages of having a child or another child, and several others talked about why they had no children. One woman senior lecturer at the teaching university said, "I love kids; it's just that circumstances have meant that I've not had kids, but I'm sure that those circumstances have a lot to do with my choice of career ... I hear these stories about how you have to coincide your pregnancies with the summer break [*laughter*] ... and about the pressure if you have to make a decision to take time off to be a mum. Will you be able to pick up? Will you be left behind?"

Neither men nor women saw children as *beneficial* to their career, although most viewed them as personally rewarding in their wider lives. A young female senior lecturer who was deciding whether to have a second child explained her dilemma: "We're feeling – well [child's name] is so great maybe we would like to have a second one ... but one of the big things is for me feeling like this has had a big impact on my publishing career, and would a second child have that impact? Would it, in fact, be sort of exponential?"

The men also mentioned that children slowed the pace of their research and promotion but tended to perceive them as a mixed blessing. A senior academic man said, "Having children is the greatest sacrifice you can make ... It's [also] the greatest blessing in some ways. It prevents you from being a single-track workaholic." In contrast, the women worried that children would truncate their career mobility due to the sheer extent of caring work. A child-free female professor articulated this very clearly: "Academic couples that I know with children, it's still seemed to be more the mother that takes on the responsibility. There are lots of variations, and I think there are lots of good husbands and partners around, but my sense is that having children has a much bigger impact on the mother ... in terms of career."

Two mothers but no fathers in the 2008 study mentioned that they had negotiated permanent part-time positions in order to manage child-rearing. One young mother at the research university who cared for extended family members as well as her own children said, "At the moment everything has to fit around my family, so it's a bit hard for me to think of a time when it's not going to be like that." Another mother at the research university spoke of children hampering her career, remarking that her parental status had "slowed [it] down considerably ... There's just the simple fact of having much less time. It's just taken me about two years to finish my book instead of, probably would have taken me about six months to finish it." At the teaching university, a mother with a junior position discussed the impact of gender and motherhood on her career: "I was very ambitious before ... When my daughter came along, I found that I wanted to spend more time with her, and it just wasn't that important any more to climb the career ladder."

The flexible hours of academic work make it possible for couples to share childcare for a few days each week, even when both work full-time. One man reported that he and his academic wife each spent one day a week working at home, during which he or she minded their youngest child. On the other three weekdays, they drove the child to an early childhood education centre, and they drove the oldest child to and from school. However, this option of sharing care is feasible only for two-parent households with flexible working hours and two careers viewed by both partners as equal.

Many academics now hire childcare services during working hours, but the need for substitute care may also arise in the evenings and weekends, when the child is sick, and especially during conferences or research trips. Mothers tended to speak the most about these kinds of dilemmas. Some could depend on the father to provide childcare, but others relied on their own mothers or other mothers when their children were sick, as well as before and after school. One single mother said, "The school that [my daughter] goes to is quite different from other schools ... There are a lot of other single mums there, so we do a lot more swapping than perhaps would happen in a normal school because we all end up in those horrific times occasionally. And like I said, on one of the times she was sick, luckily my friend's daughter was sick as well and so they were sick together."

Even though more male participants were married with children, the female subjects in the 2008 study were far more likely to discuss childcare problems. They were also more likely to say that parenting and family were central to their lives and to report that they *willingly* made work-related concessions for them. For instance, one mother in a relatively junior position said, "I do still want to be available for my daughter until she finishes school. I think there's a perception that when a child becomes a teenager, they don't need their parent any more. I find it's quite the opposite. She actually needs me more in different ways, so I'm constantly thinking about those type[s] of things. That's my main responsibility." Although some employers are willing to promote employees who accord this level of priority to family responsibilities, academics are unlikely to be promoted, especially in the research universities, unless they serve some critical cultural role in their institution or produce exceptional scholarly work.

Many of the women in the 1973 study took several years off work to have and raise their children, and then returned later to university teaching. The married mothers who worked full-time talked about the importance of efficiency in organizing their housework and childcare. Most viewed housekeeping as women's duty, although they also hired sitters and home cleaners, and some enjoyed a considerable amount of support from their mothers. In the 2008 study, fewer women reported that they had taken several *years* off to raise their children. The younger women were more likely to have taken parental leave and then hired childcare providers or enrolled their children in day care centres. A few relied on relatives to provide care while they worked at the university, but many of their relatives lived overseas or were otherwise unavailable. Finding suitable childcare remained a major concern for many women in the 2008 study, but other forms of household work were also problematic.

The Division of Housework

It is difficult to discuss housework separately from children because more housework needs to be done in a home with children, especially when they are young. However, even women without children seem to do more housework than their male counterparts. Both qualitative studies and government-sponsored time-budget studies using quantitative survey data have examined housework. Whatever methodology is employed, researchers from all the liberal states have concluded that women and especially mothers accept most of the responsibility for housekeeping even when they work full-time and that men prefer doing certain household tasks (Bittman and Pixley 1997; Craig 2006; Craig and Bittman 2008; Edlund 2007; Kitterød and Pettersen 2006; Lindsay 2008; Potuchek 1997).

Numerous studies find that academic women, especially those who become mothers, also tend to accept more responsibility for doing, organizing, or managing domestic work (Mason, Goulden, and Wolfinger 2006; O'Laughlin and Bischoff 2005). Educated men tend to do more household work than men with less education (Craig 2006; Ferber and Loeb 1997), but male academics still report less involvement in household tasks than female academics, despite flexible working hours. A study at the University of California found that women faculty between the ages of thirty and fifty who had young children reported putting in hundred-hour weeks when they included academic work, childcare, and domestic chores. In contrast, their male counterparts reported working eighty-five hours per week. In this study, the working hours of men and women did not converge until they reached the age of sixty (Mason, Goulden, and Wolfinger 2006).

Male Participants and Housework: 2008

Although few of the partnered participants in the New Zealand interviews stated that they equally shared the housework, several men initially made this claim, but most modified it after further discussion. Men who reported equal sharing tended to live with female professionals and specifically with academic women. For example, a senior academic father married to an intermediate-level academic woman said, "We share it." When the interviewer asked, "Share it fifty-fifty?" he replied, "I like to think so [*very small laugh*] but that might be disputed." There was a certain amount of nervous laughter from men relating to this question, implying that their partner might not agree with their answer. Many who reported sharing housework had no children in the household.

Several men made explicit comments about previous partner disagreements relating to the way they did particular jobs. For instance, a senior childless man who lived with a senior academic woman, said, "We share the housework fifty-fifty, but I don't do the washing because I'm incompetent at it [*laughter*]. I might wash the wrong colours together, so she's quite happy to do all of that." Other men suggested that they chose which tasks they preferred. Another childless man cohabiting with an academic woman claimed to share the housework but mentioned that he had not done much cooking since recently starting a new job. When I said, "So are you suggesting then that you divide the household tasks fairly equally?" he answered, "No, I'm suggesting that I do the things that I like doing and [my partner] does the rest [*laughter*] ... I think [she] does something along the lines of 65 percent, and I do the rest. She would probably say that it's more like 75 percent, and I do the rest." This could be seen as an example of male privilege, where women are expected to do those household tasks that men find unpleasant or less enjoyable.

Both sexes implied that a difference of opinion existed at home about how much housework the men actually did, and when and how it should be done, but some men also thought they did more than most husbands. For example, a senior lecturer father married to an academic woman stated that he did more housework than most men: "In terms of housework, we're both involved, although I would say she probably does a majority, but I don't think it's a great majority. Compared to most professional couples, I think I do more housework than your average male partner does ... We do have some issues which probably many couples have. At times, her tolerance for clutter is less than mine, you know?"

Both men and women typically remarked that the female partner did most of the domestic chores such as this lecturer father married to a homemaker: "Ah, she carries the lion's share of it. The responsibilities that fall to me are typically, um, well when I get home, I get home shortly after five, and I then take the children, she works on the preparation for the meal." Another male (full) professor, also a father, who lived with a female contract worker said, "It's probably fair to say that she does more than I do ... I think my kind of workload here, I mean, I don't normally get home till seven o'clock, so the main thing, the after-school activities, the pick-up runs, and all the rest she attends to that sort of thing ... and filling up the dishwasher and emptying that doing, doing the washing up, she tends to do most of the washing, laundry stuff. Just because she's around more in the day; I do most of the kind of the bills and that sort of stuff."

Men who were fathers, especially those living with homemakers or part-time workers, seemed least likely to share the domestic tasks equally. As one male professor living with a woman who was a part-time professional worker said, "So [*laughter in voice*] we have a, umm, a bit of a division of labour which is unbalanced: I do far less than I ought to be doing." When I asked, "So what percentage would you say you do?" he said, "Oh, probably 20 percent." To the question "And is she ok with that?" he answered, "Probably not entirely happy." This man had already told me that his wife, who once had a high-level professional job, now worked part-time.

Female Participants and Housework: 2008

The female participants in the New Zealand study reported that they shouldered the burden of housework, and many complained about doing an unequal share. A senior faculty woman from the research university who lived with her semi-retired male partner stated, "Most weekends are filled with housework ... I come back on Monday morning and some of my colleagues say, 'Have a good weekend?' and I think, what did I do on the weekend? [*laughter*] Spent most of Saturday, anyway, cleaning the place, catching up on housework ... My partner does the washing and the shopping, but I do the cooking and cleaning. He would live in a tip [dump]." Even women with male partners who were retired or semi-retired claimed to handle most domestic chores. To explain the unequal load, several women simply said they had "higher standards," and others mentioned differing levels of competence or simply said that their partner was unwilling to share the workload.

Regardless of marital status, the women participants seemed to retain most of the responsibilities for domestic work. For instance, a female senior lecturer from the teaching university lived with her frail mother and elderly uncle. She told the interviewer that she had to do the housework for everyone because her uncle pretended that he did not know how to use the equipment: "'Oh, I have no idea how to work a dishwasher,' you know, and you can show him many, many times, but he always conveniently forgets. Or, you know, 'Here are the buttons on the washing machine,' write him out instructions – 'Oh, I can't read them' [laughter]."

Several women implied that an uneven division of labour at home was a major factor in their marital separation, such as this woman senior lecturer from the teaching university: "That was one of the things that led to our separation ... I realized we'd both come home from work together and I went into the kitchen and started doing the dinner, and he sat and read the paper." Another woman from the teaching university, who described herself as a feminist, criticized women who put up with an inequitable division of labour at home: "I think it is really important that women don't just play the victim and say 'Oh my husband doesn't support me.' They have to *make* them ... I think it's actually women's responsibility to step out of these traditional gender roles."

Instances in which women did the "lion's share" of domestic labour were especially likely among older participants, parents with young children, and couples where the wife worked part-time. However, not all female participants, even those who were senior professors, complained about doing more housework than their male partner. One simply said, "When we both were working full-time, he did about half the cooking. Now that we're both practically retired, I do most of it." She did not appear to resent this. Another older woman professor said, "I don't mind [doing 80 percent of the housework] ... It really is a question of competency," suggesting that she was more efficient and skilled at cooking and cleaning. Generational differences were apparent in the division of chores, as well as differences related to women's work status and parenthood.

Making time for research and writing was perceived by many interviewees as essential for career progression. The single participants, all of whom were women, explicitly mentioned that their marital status helped in this way, whereas many mothers (but no fathers) cited the sheer amount of housework as a major reason for lower research productivity.

Family Constraints on Research-Related Travel

Research suggests that female academics are more likely than their male counterparts to change jobs for their partner's career moves (Bernard 1964; Bracken, Allen, and Dean 2006), but several women in the 2008 interviews came from overseas and were accompanied by their husband as the "trailing spouse." This kind of role reversal is becoming increasingly prevalent as universities attempt to meet their equity goals by hiring more women. All these participants reported that their (older) husband had decided to retire, live off his inheritance, work part-time, or become a consultant before he agreed to accompany them to New Zealand.

A few male subjects mentioned that they had made short-term moves for their wife's career, but this was usually seen as a temporary measure. For example, two men who were part of academic couples had held jobs in different universities and even different countries than their wife. They took leave for six months or one year in order to live with her and eventually found work in the same city. However, one of the wives accepted a job demotion in order for this to happen.

Generally, a higher proportion of male participants reported that they lived with female partners who had moved from overseas (usually from North America or the United Kingdom) to accompany them to their current university position in New Zealand. They typically downplayed the relocation consequences for the wife's employment prospects and personal/family relationships. For example, I asked a male lecturer who had recently arrived from the United States if his wife had any concerns about moving to the other side of the world. He replied, "Not really. A few concerns here and there. I mean, we'd always anticipated moving back ... but no, as I say, we both like travelling and it's not necessarily a permanent move." No mention was made of the implications for his wife's career or the distance from her friends or family.

Another senior male mentioned a previous overseas move from New Zealand to another continent, where he found a higher-ranking academic job. Apparently, his accompanying wife, who was a high-level professional, had to change professions because she was not licensed to practise in that country. When this couple later returned to New Zealand for his job, she once again changed her occupation, which he described as a "good career move" for her. Although he had reported earlier in the interview that his wife once earned more than he did, she now works part-time at a reduced salary and manages most of the domestic chores. In the 2008 interviews, accompanying wives often accepted job demotions to accommodate their husband's international career move.

The need for geographic mobility in order to find highly specialized jobs means that academics often move far away from extended family members who might otherwise have helped with childcare or domestic emergencies. Travelling for work-related reasons, with no relatives living in the same country, is particularly challenging for mothers who look after young children. A single mother from the United Kingdom, with European research interests, had recently been hired at the research university but during the interview was wondering aloud why she ever accepted the job. She said in an exasperated tone, "Taking a child as a solo mom to the UK to do research on this salary? ... It's impossible ... I don't know that I could be an international expert specializing in my area and be here [in New Zealand]."

Many of the men acknowledged the emotional and practical support they received from female partners, including their willingness to move overseas. One married father in his late thirties said, "In moving around a lot, there's always been a community base that went with me in my wife. So it wasn't going into a place completely unknown; there was a support network there, emotionally as well as financially." Another married father in his early thirties said, "My wife has always been very supportive of my career ... She can easily find work, you know, wherever she arrives or wherever we go."

As I noted in Chapter 4, academics sometimes strategically use job offers from other institutions to gain job permanence, more money, or more research leave at their current university, or simply to find better positions elsewhere. One highly productive female lecturer discussed how she obtained her permanent position at the research university, after working there on a temporary contract: "Well I actually had a job offer from another university right around the time when my contract expired ... So when that came near to its end, I applied for other jobs and I received a job offer, but I didn't really want to leave, and so I went to the [academic manager] and said, you know, I want to stay but I have another job offer, so I'll go unless you offer me something permanent. So that's when they offered me the permanent position." Her husband worked in a profession that could have accommodated her relocation, and she believed that she could have persuaded him to leave the country, if necessary. However, not all academics could tempt their partners to relocate.

Many participants in my 2008 study acknowledged that they could improve their professional circumstances if they moved overseas, but those with partners and children sometimes doubted that they could accept any job, because their partner would refuse to move or their children's education and friendships would be disrupted. One senior woman (partnered, with two children) spoke bitterly of a recent denial of promotion in her university and her intention to apply for a more senior posting at another university in a distant city. When questioned about the feasibility of relocating her family, she doubted that her semi-retired partner would agree to move: "There would be a problem [*laughter*]. I ... we'd have to ... I don't know, I can't answer that ... Yeah, I ... I don't know what would happen. That's, sort of like, in the world of speculation at this stage." In contrast, more of the men *assumed* that their partner would agree to move if they received a promotional position at another university.

Despite this gendered finding, several men in the 2008 interviews expressed concern about lack of geographic mobility, perhaps because they expected eventual promotion to professor (discussed in Chapter 6), and more were headhunted for overseas jobs. One ambitious senior lecturer, a father married to a career-oriented academic woman, conveyed this quite plainly: "I've been offered lots of jobs overseas, but I can't take them. It's not an option ... If I wasn't married with kids, I would have left here three years ago." Another lecturer, a father whose wife was about to return to paid work after extended parental leave, said with sadness in his voice, "A year ago, I was offered a job [overseas] that in many ways I would have been keen to take ... Then we found out that we had another child on the way, and that meant we would only have a single income [in an expensive location]. So I ended up turning that job down."

Family constraints on improving one's job prospects were clearly a bone of contention for many participants. A male professor talked about the possibility of moving overseas for a job. When I asked him explicitly if the move would have posed a problem for his wife's career, he said, "I suppose it would have because it was the time when she had employment here. But we were just willing to face that, if it happened ... She would have been willing to try something else." Although we do not know his wife's view on relocating, his comments provide another example of the assumption that men's careers should be granted priority in the household.

Several women (but no men) seemed unaware that receiving an overseas job offer could be used as a career-enhancing bargaining tool, and almost all of them expressed disapproval of such tactics. The men were more likely to perceive that they had career prospects overseas, but fathers partnered with female professionals particularly lamented the family constraints that hindered them from accepting these advancement opportunities. A few male participants married to academics saw relocation as a joint venture, such as this senior man working at the research university: "We're not going to make a move unless both of us do well ... We don't actually want to move, but if we do, we move as a couple." However, the last time this man had an overseas promotional possibility, his academic wife could not find a job in the same city, and he had to reject the offer. Nonetheless, he reassured me that turning down the job was acceptable to him because his current university had a higher international ranking than the one making the offer.

In contrast, women seemed more inclined to focus on their duties at work and at home, and only two reported being recruited by a personnel agency or colleague to apply for an overseas position. Perhaps this can be explained by women's more junior rank and their lower social capital as academics.

Conclusion

My two studies, and the research from the liberal states, suggest that the gender gap in academia is partly perpetuated by family circumstances and the household division of labour, as well as institutional and collegial factors. Statistically, we have seen throughout this book that more academic men than women are married parents living in two-parent households, and female partners tend to be younger, have lower employment attachments, and work shorter hours for pay. Married academic mothers with young children are much more likely than married fathers to hold part-time, temporary, or junior positions. The fact that a disproportionate percentage of tenured and senior academic women are single, divorced, and childless is another indication of the difficulties of integrating work and family for women. Considerable research shows that women who combine full-time academic careers with motherhood continue to face tremendous challenges in terms of working hours, stress levels, and work-family conflict, especially when they become single mothers (Monroe et al. 2008; Rosser 2004).

Although more women have joined the workforce in recent decades, the division of domestic chores remains unequal in many homes, even when both partners develop demanding professional careers. Women with fewer or no children are still more likely than mothers with several children to reach the highest ranks, and academic women who are promoted to the senior ranks more often remain single, become separated or divorced, and produce fewer children than they might otherwise have chosen. Those who become mothers typically work harder than men to balance family responsibilities with paid employment. Regardless of educational qualifications and occupational prestige, women are more likely than men to fit their paid work around the needs of their partner, children, parents, and other family members. Sometimes this is done for perceived necessity, such as keeping their marriage together or because alternative support is unavailable.

Partnered women and mothers also accept more *responsibility* than their male partners for allocating, managing, and supervising these tasks. This relates to gendered expectations and sometimes to personal preferences, but someone must clean the house and care for children and frail parents. Caregiving may enrich women's lives, but it also limits their time and energy to devote to career advancement, to engage in social or leisure activities, and to sleep. Heavy care responsibilities could either modify women's ambition and research productivity or require them to become super-efficient in their work habits.

To counteract the gendered relations at home, university mentoring programs may need to examine these issues more openly, including how to prioritize tasks and manage time. More importantly, academic women and their colleagues, friends, and partners need to consider and discuss the implications of their division of labour at home, including the personal satisfactions as well as the potential career penalties. The research from the liberal states clearly shows that family circumstances still matter to women's academic careers, although there are many variations by jurisdiction and household. Nevertheless, meaningful change in the allocation of domestic chores will require complex negotiations between partners and within households.

Subjectivities and the Gender Gap **6**

Men are hung up on the success ethic. Maybe women are too – once they get into academia and get caught on the treadmill of publishing.

– FEMALE DOCTORAL STUDENT, CANADA, 1975

At times with certain male colleagues, I have to find strategies to assert my place. There are a couple of situations where I don't feel listened to because I'm a woman.

– FEMALE LECTURER, NEW ZEALAND, 2008

In the previous chapter, we saw that the domestic circumstances and division of labour often vary considerably for male and female academics. Despite improvements to women's educational attainment and labour force participation, many women still prioritize their partner's career, do the housework, and accept most of the responsibility for the daily care of young children (England 2010). The research also suggests that perceptions of work and family responsibilities tend to vary by gender. This chapter focuses on the subjectivities of male and female scholars, how they vary according to socioeconomic circumstances, and how they could influence the academic gender gap.

Professional success is often attributed to intelligence and hard work but also to being organized, knowing the right people, feeling comfortable with colleagues, wanting to gain promotion, and projecting professional confidence. Throughout the book, I have referred to this as social capital. The desire to reach the top of one's profession, the subjective belief that one is an expert, and the willingness and ability to act on this belief tend to be learned behaviour. Career ambition and self-confidence are often developed via early encouragement throughout childhood but also from career mentoring, positive collegial relations, and favourable job-related experiences. Expectations of a fulfilling personal life and work-life balance also influence career commitment.

Gendered Perceptions of Academics and Academia

Perceptions of Academia: 1973

Participants in the Canadian study were explicitly asked if they considered themselves to be "successful" in their careers and were later questioned about indicators of success and whether they believed that these were gendered. Although the interviewees were divided between those who mentioned extrinsic and intrinsic criteria of occupational success, more of the younger women focused on extrinsic criteria such as rank, salary, and publications, and reported fewer gender differences. However, a number of participants suggested that men were more interested than women in trying to improve their rank, salary, and status, such as this woman in science who said, "Men seem terribly hooked on titles. I think they are thinking of their obituaries" (Baker 1975, 191).

Is there any evidence that men are more interested than women in getting ahead on the job? If such is the case, they might expend more effort learning the rules of the game and seeking tangible rewards such as promotion or collegial recognition. However, willingness to pursue rewards might also relate to high achievement motivation or feeling comfortable with occupational values. In the 1973 study, several women suggested that men actively seek recognition and remuneration more than women do but also that men's actions and efforts are perceived differently by others. For example, an assistant professor in physical education implied that men in her department insisted on being paid for all their work at the university: "Male professors in physical education get paid for more things, such as coaching. Women don't make demands for extra money like the men" (ibid., 210). An associate professor in science went even further: "Women are not promoted at the same rate as men, and perhaps rationalize this by saying that they are more interested in teaching. The women do the scutty work in the labs and get no credit for it. It's a housekeeping role. Whether they enjoy these jobs or just rationalize their poor position, I don't know" (ibid., 193).

Several interviewees mentioned that academic women's competence, credibility, and worth were questioned more than men's by both students and colleagues, especially when women entered a new academic environment. For instance, an assistant professor in the social sciences said, "You have to prove yourself for the first few weeks – prove that you know the material. This is not difficult to do – just a waste of time!" A full professor suggested that women's voices were not taken seriously in committee meetings: "If a woman says something at a meeting, it is often ignored until a man repeats the same idea and everyone thinks it's wonderful." For that reason, she reported, she seldom spoke at meetings anymore (ibid., 132).

A major complaint of these participants was that women academics in this Canadian university were not recognized as competent unless they were actually *better* than their male colleagues. Interviewees in the lower ranks and temporary appointments most often repeated these kinds of comments, such as this female doctoral student in the humanities: "Female professors have to publish more and better articles and have to have more and better graduate students to receive any recognition. If they don't do this, they are treated with patriarchal tolerance, but they don't exist as far as major decision-making in the department" (ibid., 132). Another woman who had dropped out of the doctoral program justified her decision to leave academia by saying, "You had to be on the top if you were female, even though they would accept a mediocre man" (ibid., 197).

This differential treatment perceived by many female academics, combined with the paucity of positive role models, led junior women to doubt whether they would ever reach a senior position. In addition, a few participants clearly questioned their own intellectual or professional abilities. For example, a young doctoral student in medicine who was close to graduation and planning an academic career said that she did not think she could "handle" the job of assistant professor (ibid., 140). Although there were no men to form a comparison group in this study, it is unlikely that a male doctoral student would have said this in the 1970s, or now.

Perceptions of Academia: 2008

In the New Zealand study, participants were asked if they thought that their gender had any impact on their career. Most men seemed genuinely puzzled by this question, usually saying that they had not given it much thought. The typical male response was, "Never really thought about it [pause]. It's not something I've ever really given a huge amount of thought to." The men's answers to this question generally differed from those of the women, who reported numerous instances of what they saw as social exclusion from collegial networks, a systematic devaluing of their work, and institutional discrimination against mothers with young children. The men who *had* given the subject some thought typically lived with academic women, and several told stories of their partner's negative work experiences. This suggests that they saw gender as an issue affecting female academics but not necessarily themselves. For example, one man who was a senior lecturer said, "When [my partner] took up the job at [X] University [in New Zealand], the number of obstacles that existed because she was not part of the network of men was enormous. They made her life extremely uncomfortable, which was part of why we ended up shifting up here [to Auckland]." The implication of this comment was that his wife quit her job because of her negative experiences with male colleagues.

When men talked about their own lives, they were seldom able to pinpoint any problem or even specific advantages to being a male in the university workplace. One male lecturer at the research university said, "Mm. Well, I assume that things are probably easier for me than it would be for a woman coming through, but I wouldn't be able to say how ... You sort of assume that the white man is getting the easy ride through the system." A senior lecturer at the research university, who was also involved in the faculty union, said, "I've always just assumed that I have enjoyed some advantage or privilege as a result of being male – you know, in the job market and maybe even in career advancement – but it's something you just don't really think about that much." One of the most explicit recognitions of the impact of gender came from a senior man married to a feminist academic, in reminiscing about his doctoral school experiences in the United States: "I've never reflected on that, but I think it probably has ... I think my doctoral university department was quite a male kind of culture when I was there in those years [1980s]. And I think that is definitely the truth where I was doing my tenure track at [X] University [in the United States]. There were some women in the department, but it was a bit of a boys club. There was quite a lot of *boysie*-type stuff [small laugh]." Even younger men, those involved in union activities, and men married to academic women tended to see gender as something related to women's careers rather than their own.

In the 2008 interviews, the female participants made numerous comments about the gendered nature of the university workplace or their observations that men and women were treated differently. However, most of these remarks related to colleagues' reactions to academic women who were mothers, rather than the impact of gender alone. Nevertheless, several suggested that women more often seek approval from their colleagues but do not always receive it, such as this senior woman: "It's the reality – we all know this, don't we – that your accomplishments will not be celebrated. I mean, you know that perfectly well ... And it's discouraging particularly to younger women. And it's possible, of course, that our socialization means that we do seek more approval or have more anxiety about not getting it."

The New Zealand interviewees were also asked about the best and worst part of the job. For the worst part, many mentioned the growing bureaucracy, administrative reporting, and neo-liberal restructuring, but some also implied that they felt marginalized in their chosen profession. Several seemed to view their colleagues as undesirable people and made disparaging comments about them. For example, one male senior lecturer from the teaching university, who entered academia late in life after working in a skilled labour job, said, "I have a problem with the cronyism in academic departments and in academic life." Women also made negative remarks about their colleagues, such as a single mother and senior lecturer in the research university who talked about the "massive egos" of her male colleagues: "In academia you find eccentric people who can be difficult sometimes. I think the most difficult thing I find about academia without a doubt is what I see to be injustices in the system ... I think there are a lot of people who pad up their work big time and they put, like, a showcase out to the dean saying, 'This is what I'm doing and it's so wonderful and fabulous and I'm top of the class' – and they're not." These observations were typically made by individuals who positioned themselves as outsiders or were treated as such by colleagues, a category that seemed to be over-populated by women in the middle and lower ranks, people with working-class or cultural minority backgrounds, and those who had failed to receive an expected promotion.

Unlike the subjects of the 1973 study, most 2008 participants – both men and women – reported feeling comfortable in academia, saying that they loved the lifestyle and enjoyed the intellectual environment. When asked what they saw as the best part of the job, most talked about the high value placed on intellectual autonomy, the opportunities to research their own specialized topics, and the chance to read and write in areas of their own choosing. Others mentioned the opportunity to challenge students' minds and watch them progress.

Senior academics briefly discussed the pleasure of teaching, but most focused on research and publishing. For example, a senior woman said, "Well, the research and writing would have to be top of the list. I actually enjoy being part of an academic community as well ... You know, if I had half the teaching load, I would enjoy it twice as much [*small laugh*]." Another senior woman made a similar comment: "Probably the research or the writing ... Doing my own research is satisfying ... but I also enjoy the contact with students, particularly graduate students." Men made similar statements, such as this senior academic who said, "I know there are times when I am teaching or doing stuff that I think that it's amazing that someone pays me to do this ... Well it's funny but I actually get an enormous amount of satisfaction out of seeing students do well. That's a big part of the pleasure of it. But ah – the publishing and seeing work in print or seeing people cite my stuff."

In contrast, more of the junior and intermediate academics discussed other aspects of the job, such as teaching and flexibility for family time. For instance, a single mother who was a lecturer said, "I love pushing people to achieve great things and to challenge their minds ... I love the crazy people and having my own office and looking after the students and doing my own little funny work and my writings and things. I love the flexibility of it that if [my child] does get sick, then I can take a day off and it's not going to throw anyone completely out of whack, you know, if I don't have a teaching day." Her view of her research – "my own little funny work" – was quite different from most men's perceptions of their research. A similar comment about flexibility for family responsibilities was made by an intermediate-ranking father, married to another academic, although this was an unusual remark for a man to make: "One of the privileges of being a university academic is that we have work schedules ... that are not conventional in terms of a nine-to-five job. So what [my wife] and I do, we arrange our teaching schedules in family-friendly ways." Even those who had not been promoted far in the academic hierarchy valued the flexible hours and intellectual freedom, such as this older male who said, "I like teaching, I like being at a university, I like the reading, I like the research, I like books [*laughter*]. I like thinking."

Research suggests that academic men are more likely than academic women to view the university promotional system as fair and to experience fewer dilemmas about the long work hours required to succeed, about harassment from managers or colleagues, exclusion from networks, or work-family conflict (Carr et al. 2000; Seagram, Gould, and Pyke 1998). Perhaps it is relevant to note that academic men also enjoy more domestic support from parents and partners (Bassett 2005). All these factors influence confidence levels and expectations of reaching the top of the profession.

Expectations of Reaching the Highest Ranks

As questions on reaching the highest rank were not explicitly asked in the 1973 interviews, this section focuses on the 2008 study from New Zealand. In it, participants of both sexes cited promotion setbacks they or their colleagues had experienced and their belief that the promotion system was rigorous and challenging. Mothers from the research university particularly mentioned these concerns, reporting that the promotion system made it too hard to reach the top. Several male interviewees from the teaching university stated that promotion was definitely easier there than at the research university, particularly for applicants with few publications but strong teaching and service records.

The largest difference between men and women related to the question about promotion to professor (equivalent to senior full professor in North America), which was phrased "Do you expect to reach the rank of professor by the time you retire?" This question was asked toward the end of the interview, after various aspects of career history and family circumstances were discussed. In reply, women in junior and intermediate ranks generally expressed low expectations of reaching the top, and most answered with an immediate and resounding "no!" After some prompting from the interviewer, they gave a variety of reasons for this, including their own lack of intelligence, lack of ambition, insufficient time or energy, insufficient publications, lack of respect from colleagues, and no desire for additional administrative or managerial responsibilities (Baker 2010a). To clarify, it is now possible to become a professor in New Zealand without accepting responsibility for administrative or managerial positions such as head of department.

Women's Expectations of Promotion to Professor: 2008

Most of the junior and intermediate women (lecturers and senior lecturers) viewed their promotional prospects far less favourably than men of a comparable rank. In fact, the follow-up discussions relating to this issue revealed much about the gendered subjectivities or identities of these participants. First, several women openly suggested that they were not ambitious enough or smart enough, such as this single mother at the research university: "No! I don't think I'm ambitious enough. I don't think I have enough ... I don't know that I can. I just don't think I'm clever enough." When I reminded her that she had previously been awarded a doctoral scholarship, she replied, "Yeah, but that was for the PhD." I asked her how far she thought she would be promoted, and she replied, "I don't know. Senior lecturer maybe." When I reminded her that she was already a senior lecturer at the age of thirty-five, she revised her statement: "Yeah. I don't know, maybe associate professor."

Other women suggested that they were too busy even to contemplate applying for promotion, such as this mother of three children who also had responsibilities for her dying mother, her mother-in-law, and some nieces and nephews: "It's not even in my vocab [to aspire to professor] – it's not in the kind of mental reference I have for where I'm going. I can plan a month ahead but beyond that, it's just kind of in the ether." In reply to the question of whether they expected to reach the professoriate before retirement, some women actually denigrated the kinds of academic activities that lead to promotion, such as this childless woman in her late thirties at the teaching university: "No ... I don't see myself jumping through hoops for academia and publishing research and doing all that stuff over the next twenty years ... I've got other interests." She mentioned that these included fiction writing, which she saw as more personally rewarding than writing academic articles in peer-reviewed journals "that no one reads."

Other women said that they had no ambition to take on leadership roles, such as this senior lecturer at the teaching university, who was already in her fifties. However, she also mentioned that she had insufficient publications for promotion: "No ... I don't really have that ambition. I don't really want to be in that kind of leadership role. I like what I'm doing. I like contact with the students, so I don't want to be out of the classroom and just doing kind of administration and head of school and, you know, that kind of thing ... I mean I would probably work towards associate professor, but I don't think before I retire I would be likely to have enough published to qualify as a professor."

Several participants made similar comments, such as an older woman in an intermediate position at the teaching university. She stated that she did not want to do administrative work but also reminded the interviewer that her academic career started late in life. However, several younger childless women at the intermediate rank suggested that being a professor (especially combined with head of department) was not always a desirable job, especially for a woman. A woman in this category at the teaching university said, "A female associate professor who recently left and has gone back [overseas] said that she actually found it a real burden because she was expected to take on all the scut work that the blokes at that level didn't want ... I mean they limit the amount that you can teach, but the other duties that come on top of it she found quite onerous ... I'd be quite happy just getting to the top of senior lecturer." Even the women senior professors claimed that they had not really expected to reach that level, because they did not see themselves as experts or did not think that their work was taken seriously by colleagues or managers. Some senior women mentioned that they gained promotion simply by working hard or "being in the right place at the right time." Still others reported negative consequences upon reaching the professoriate, such as additional criticism, loneliness, or lack of friends.

Australians and New Zealanders often talk about the "tall poppy syndrome," suggesting that successful people who stand out above the crowd are not always well liked and are therefore cut down or criticized by colleagues and associates. Even though no interview questions dealt with this, several women mentioned that ambitious academics, especially women, are often viewed as tall poppies. For example, a senior academic woman from the research university, originally from the United Kingdom, expressed concern about this syndrome, suggesting that it was particularly stringent for senior women: "Climbing the ladder is a mixed experience, particularly for women, but I find in Australia and New Zealand it's a rather mixed experience for everybody because the more you climb, the more a target you become and the less support you get. I mean, I think the tall poppy thing cuts across gender, but I just think that people find it easier to resent senior women for being there than they find men a problem [ironic laugh]."

Other senior women suggested that they applied for a professorial position only because someone urged them to, but they had not expected to obtain the job or promotion. Two strong themes among the female participants regarding impediments to promotion to professor were lack of confidence in their academic abilities and feelings of obligation to others (usually family members). Both these themes are apparent in the following life story of a senior woman, who explained how she became a full professor at the research university in New Zealand: "No ... I don't think I thought I was either clever enough or the right kind of person [to become a professor]. I was much too shy ... It just wasn't really on my horizon, I think." When asked "Okay, and how do you explain that it happened? How did you get to be a professor?" she replied,

> Hard work and perseverance, and a little bit of being at the right place at the right time, I think. Yeah, that is my explanation ... Somebody wrote me a note [when I worked in the United States] and said, "Apply for this [professorial] job," and I said, "You've got to be kidding!" but I applied ... It was a way of coming back to New Zealand, to be perfectly frank, having a look, and I did not at all expect to be offered the job. And when I was offered the job, I felt I couldn't refuse, because I would then have come back under false pretences ... Well, I came back to interview for the job, with expenses paid, so there was an ethical dilemma around that. In a sense, I felt slightly panicked at the offer ... because I wasn't sure if I was competent and because I wasn't absolutely sure I was ready to leave my [grown-up] children and [separated] husband [both remaining in the USA].

Women's stories about their reluctance to strive for or accept professorial positions, including the one above, often referred to the circumstances and well-being of other family members, especially children, husbands, and even ex-husbands.

Another senior woman at the research university said she applied for promotion to professor only because a senior manager urged her to do so but added that she would have been satisfied to remain an associate professor. When I asked her, "Did you ever think throughout your career that you would reach the top of the profession?" she replied, "I didn't, no. During the eighties when I could not get promoted, I was extremely depressed, and when finally I managed to get an associate professorship I believed that this was the furthest I was going to get, and I was by no means unhappy about the thought that, you know, I'd managed to get an associate professorship. But that was fine." I asked, "And so then you only applied for full professor when someone suggested it to you? If he hadn't suggested it, you wouldn't have done it?" She answered, "No, I wouldn't. I thought that I didn't have enough books on my publication list ... No, I'd reached the level of promotion that I would have been happy to rest with."

A few female lecturers or senior lecturers did aspire to rise in the profession, such as this married mother with strong spousal and parental support, who had graduated from a prestigious overseas institution and now worked at the research university: "I definitely would like to become at least an associate professor. I'd be disappointed if I didn't get that far." Another female lecturer from the teaching university denied being ambitious but later mentioned that she wanted equity: "I've applied for a promotion [to senior lecturer], but I'm not so conscious of wanting to climb the ladder as such but on the basis of my relative worth, you know, just to be fair ... fair dues."

Several women interviewees and one man at the research university suggested that some women were convincing each other that promotion was too difficult, including members of the university's mentoring group for women. For example, a childless woman from the research university, with a local doctorate, said, "I think I have the ability to get to professor, but I've heard that it is very difficult." When I asked her who had told her this, she said "other women." However, the research university's equity committee insists that the proportion of women receiving promotion is not lower than the percentage of applicants, although women *are* less likely than men to apply. This has also been found in Australian research (Probert 2005). This suggests that if more female academics were encouraged to apply for promotion, more could be promoted.

Men's Expectations of Promotion to Professor: 2008

In contrast to the women, the men in the New Zealand study expressed more confidence about reaching the professoriate, which they saw as a normal, desirable, and attainable aspiration. None suggested that it would involve too much work or responsibility or would result in unwanted consequences such as isolation or loss of friends. In fact, most reported that they *assumed* they would be promoted if they continued working at their current pace, and some senior men had always expected to reach the top. For example, a married male who was a lecturer at the research university answered the question about becoming a professor before retirement in this way: "Yeah. Probably. Hopefully in the long term ... I mean I'm not shooting for promotion at every turn, but if I publish at a reasonable rate and teach." Another male lecturer, also a married father under thirty-five, said, "I actively work under the assumption ... My suspicion would be to publish lots and become incredibly respected and an influential member of the [disciplinary] fraternity ... Yeah, I assume that I'll do well until somebody starts to tell me otherwise." An associate professor, who was a married father in his mid-forties, said, "I would like it to happen within the next two to three years ... I think that it *will* happen." These comments from men display much more confidence than those from the female subjects.

Only three male participants openly doubted that they would ever reach the professoriate. Two male senior lecturers had received their PhDs or entered academia after working in other occupations and acknowledged that they had insufficient time before retirement to reach the top of the hierarchy. One was a partnered but childless man over fifty who worked at the research university. He responded to the question about promotion to professor with, "Probably not ... Well, I'm likely to retire in fifteen years ... I don't have enough years. I'm much more productive in terms of teaching. I like the teaching and I don't think that's actually where the promotions are." Another man, a father married to an academic, claimed he wanted a more balanced life and was not prepared to work the necessary hours to gain promotion, which he said amounted to eighty hours a week. However, he also admitted that he did not think he was a good enough scholar to become a professor:

> My track record so far in terms of my scholarly output I think has been slow, for reasons of my own ability but also the time that I've given over to teaching ... I'm trying to wean myself away from excessive preparation in terms of my teaching. And I think also getting to the point of your study – I think being a parent ... in a relationship with a full-time academic, our time is necessarily limited in terms of what we can put into research and producing scholarly output, which in the end gets you to the professorial rank ... We want to spend time

with our kids; we don't want to put in eighty-hour weeks and if it takes eighty-hour weeks to become a professor, well then, okay I'm happy not being a professor.

It may be relevant that two of the three men who did not expect to be promoted were childless, and all three were partnered with academic women, which could reduce the social pressure on them to become the main household earner. Certainly, the kinds of remarks that they made were much more prevalent among the female participants.

Generally, the interviews showed that most of the men expected to reach the top of the profession, whereas most of the women either doubted that they would or expressed surprise that they had. It is possible, however, that many women in New Zealand feel that it is socially unacceptable to admit professional confidence to another academic, even though they are willing to talk about success in other aspects of their lives, such as friendships or mothering skills. However, many of these women were raised or educated overseas.

Another explanation for women's low confidence is that they experience more constraints on promotion than men do. Many women receive less recognition and support for their careers or their particular research projects from their colleagues but also from their parents, partners, and extended families. Mothers with young children are typically time poor, and many lack partner support with domestic chores. Several women also mentioned that they lacked a quiet private space to work at home. One extreme example from the 2008 interviews was reported by a female lecturer with a working-class background, who had created a home office. However, when her mother-in-law moved in with them, the other family members expected her to work in a corner of the living room, where the television was located. Apparently, they did not take her career seriously, but overcrowding and low household income also precluded her from retaining a suitable workspace at home.

Regardless of the reason for low promotional expectations, most female participants from both studies said that when they looked at their colleagues, they saw few women at the top, which gave them a powerful message. The few women who did hold senior academic positions seemed overworked and under-acknowledged, and they sometimes lacked the kind of personal lives that many young women see as normal and desirable (married with children).

Gender and the Desire for Children

In the previous chapter, we saw that more academic women than men remain childless, believing that motherhood could potentially damage their career. However, parenthood is often associated with maturity, normality, and adulthood, and it tends to be central to the identity of both men and women (Baker 2005; Dykstra 2006; Gillespie 2003). The two sets of interviews showed some notable changes over time in attitudes toward children and careers, but they also revealed some similarities.

Academics and Children: 1973

The 1970s tended to foster strong social expectations that married adults should reproduce, that mothers should be the primary carers of children, and that they should look after their children at home at least until they entered school. Consequently, most mothers from that era gave priority to their family over their career, especially when their children were preschoolers. In the Canadian study, for example, one temporary lecturer reported that she stayed at home for eighteen years to raise three children, admitting that she would have felt guilty had she not done so. She added, "My husband was never interested in domestic things or children, but I knew that when I married him and accepted it" (Baker 1975, 176).

At the same time, the 1973 participants worried that taking time off work to have and raise children would be detrimental to their career. For instance, one mother of three children who was in her fifties and working in an intermediate position in the science faculty said, "You never know if you will lose your seniority or if it will affect your publications if you take time off to have children." This woman had experienced problems finding a permanent academic job because her husband was a professor and anti-nepotism rules had initially prevented a full-time appointment for her. Not until she and her husband divorced was she given a permanent position and a pay raise – almost as though her single status were proof of her renewed career commitment (ibid., 130).

A few mothers in the 1973 study stated that they accorded priority to their family, as did this assistant professor in education: "I haven't been interested in pursuing a 'career.' I'm not the upwardly mobile type. I haven't put my career first ... I do what I have to do but my career is not my whole life. My family value is worth something" (ibid., 177). In contrast, most participants, especially those who were single and child-less, were more likely to say that their careers were very important to them, even though some struggled to achieve success.

Academics and Children: 2008

In the 2008 study, the concern that children might ruin their career remained a common theme among the women but *not* the men. Part of women's apprehension about having children related to the enduring social expectation that they would become the main carers but also to the changing nature of their job requirements. University-based aca-demics are now continually expected to initiate new projects and find publishers to disseminate their research, even when they retain heavy family responsibilities. For example, a single and childless woman was about to apply for tenure but was also considering her personal future at the time of the interview. When asked about her personal plans, she said, "How would I ever have time to have kids? I find this job hard enough as it is, without having kids as well ... I haven't had time to de-velop relationships, to actually get married and have kids. So I guess the nature of the job, and the fact that it's obviously very time consuming, and if you're ambitious you focus on that, so you kind of knock out the social activities."

Only one man admitted that he and his female partner might want to remain childless. This man, who worked at the teaching university and was partnered with an academic woman at another university, discussed their ambivalence about becoming parents: "Being childless allows us a little bit more freedom to burn the candle at both ends when we need to take the appropriate amount of down time ... I've got a great amount of admiration for anyone who has children in this particular game, because I think it is an extra burden, I think it is harder."

Several women, but no men, reported unapologetically that they *never* wanted children. A senior woman with an academic partner said, "I've never, ever in my life, ever wanted children." She went on to say, "I've never felt like [having children] is something women *have to do* ... And the fact is, I don't think I'm that well suited to having children, and it doesn't bother me that I don't ... One of the nice things about the job that we have is that it actually contains a lot of freedom to follow one's interests and direct one's own time. And as a writer and a creative person, I think, well, that's where my creative energies go and I think that's fine." She also commented on the difficulty of combining childrearing with an academic career: "I could never have imagined pursuing a career if I had had children ... I could not have found time to bring up children ... I think I probably would have liked at least one child if I'd had enough money to have a nanny but [*laughter*] not otherwise."

In the 2008 study, mothers also expressed more concern than fathers about leaving their children with a caregiver during work-related travel. A partnered mother at the research university noted that travel grants were given only to scholars whose sabbaticals involved travelling over-seas for at least six weeks and asserted that this limitation discriminated against mothers with young children. She claimed that she couldn't take her school-aged children with her, but she also firmly stated, "I've never been away from my children for more than two weeks, and I have no desire to do so now," a comment that no male participant made.

A senior woman suggested that both she and one of her children suffered psychologically when she travelled alone for work reasons. She talked about the emotional difficulty of travelling without her family, even though her semi-retired partner appeared to do a fair amount of childcare:

> With my first sabbatical, it was too expensive to take the family ... I went away for two months. You think in ideal terms that this would be fantastic, in all the work you can get done, but I was incredibly lonely. I *really* missed my family. I found it quite strange in fact, especially the weekends ... I've had subsequent sabbaticals and I've gotten a lot better. I think I miss them a lot more than they miss me, to be honest. But having said that, when I first started going away on my own, [my son] did become a lot more clingy, and every time I was subsequently going away, it was harder and harder for him rather than the other way around. So [my career] has affected him.

Several men implied that they missed their family while on sabbatical, but none suggested that their children could be damaged by their work-related absences from home. These kinds of comments were made exclusively by mothers.

The Desire for Work-Life Balance

Both men and women report the desire for more balance between their paid work and the rest of their lives (Duxbury and Higgins 2000; OECD 2007a). Particularly those employees who are required to work long hours, who hold multiple jobs, earn low wages, and retain daily caring responsibilities express concern about the shortage of time to complete their work, enjoy family or leisure activities, or simply relax. Even employees with adequate earnings say that they feel time poor. However, women, and especially mothers with young children, are more likely than men or fathers to raise these points (OECD 2007a). Academics are also concerned about work-life balance, with more women than men commenting on the negative effect of work stress on family life (Bassett 2005; Bracken, Allen, and Dean 2006; Kinman and Jones 2004; O'Laughlin and Bischoff 2005). This includes the necessity of working long hours, the absence of suitable childcare services (especially infant and after-school care), and job requirements to travel.

However, we need to keep two factors in mind. First, stress levels are not always related to the actual workload but rather to expectations, perceptions, and levels of social support. Even so, stress is particularly elevated in academia when research productivity needs to be high during the pre-tenure years to retain a job and gain employment security. Women are often in their prime childbearing years when they apply for tenure (O'Laughlin and Bischoff 2005). Few gender differences have been found in perceptions of partner support for academic careers, as many women live with academic men who are senior to them and who provide career advice and a sounding board for intellectual ideas (ibid.). Sweet and Moen (2002) found that co-working in an academic setting tends to buffer work and family strain, especially when partners are employed at the same university. However, married or partnered mothers perceive lower levels of partner support for parenting and domestic work than fathers do.

More academic women than men live alone and become single parents, with no other adult in the household to share the domestic workload (Bassett 2005; Bracken, Allen, and Dean 2006; Brooks 1997). Academic women's higher separation/divorce rate may reflect the unusual level of assertiveness of women with PhDs, including their unwillingness to accept perceived inequities within marriage. It could also be explained by the stress of working long hours, although academic men work longer hours than women and have lower divorce rates. The higher divorce rate of academic women could simply reflect their greater opportunities to become self-supporting compared to other women, as well as their strong career orientation in a world that still expects women to become the main care provider in the household.

Second, the findings on perceptions of workload and stress are also influenced by participants' willingness to admit coping problems to researchers. Women tend to reveal that they experience stress problems at work or at home more freely than men do (Alvesson and Billing 2009). Nevertheless, we have already seen that family circumstances vary for male and female academics, which partly explains gendered perceptions. After all, family stress and work stress are interrelated.

Work-Life Balance: 1973

In the Canadian interviews, many participants spoke of problems balancing their academic work with their family life. In 1971, the Canadian government had instigated a fifteen-week paid maternity leave for all eligible employees under the Unemployment Insurance Program, but the university where the interviews took place offered no additional maternity/parental leave (Baker 1975, 1995, 89). As noted earlier, it had also adopted an anti-nepotism rule that prevented many married interviewees from securing full-time academic jobs if their male partner was already employed there.

During the early 1970s, mothers were typically expected to care for young children at home, and some of the interviewees did this for years before beginning or resuming their academic careers. In addition, many had relocated to Canada from the United States and seldom had family members living close by to share the care work. Few public childcare services were available in western Canada at the time, but some mothers managed to develop successful academic careers through efficient household management, hard work, partner support, and hired help. However, these women were not always seen as positive role models by their younger female students and colleagues, as they had to work so hard. Although many policies and attitudes have changed since the 1970s, the female academics in the 2008 study also reported problems with work-life balance.

Work-Life Balance: 2008

Several participants in the 2008 interviews, both men and women, labelled themselves as "workaholics" or reported working most of the time, including evenings and weekends. When asked if her marital status had influenced her career in any way, a senior woman who was single and childless said, "For sure – it's much easier to be a workaholic if you're single." To the question "Would you see yourself as a workaholic?" she replied, "Oh – definitely! Yes, I think that you *have* to be; I think that academic life attracts fairly compulsive personalities. I think that we're all a bit obsessive." It was unusual for women to calmly admit to researchers that their job overwhelmed their life, as this one did. Although both men and women reported a desire for work-life balance, few men seemed prepared to reduce their working hours, especially if they might forfeit promotional opportunities.

In contrast, a number of the women reported that they lowered their career ambitions after childbirth, worked half-time, took employment leave, accepted caring responsibility for children and relatives, or relocated with their partner's job. Several also expressed guilt about not spending enough time with their children earlier in their careers. For example, a successful senior woman reminisced, "When I look back, I regret not being able to spend more time with the children when they were little." No male participants made that sort of comment.

In the 2008 interviews, a woman in her late thirties provided an extreme example of a well-qualified female academic in a permanent position who granted a great deal of priority to family. She had recently joined the research university in a part-time but tenure-stream position and had been able to negotiate this because her area of expertise was in great demand, and she was highly recommended as a productive researcher and excellent teacher. When I asked her later in the interview about the possibility of moving to another university to gain a better position, she said,

> I cannot take promotional positions with a terminally ill mother, not with young children, not with the in-laws, you know? There is no room for that kind of expansion in my career. And I don't think that's the way I'd like to go anyway. I wouldn't want the job to be the overriding thing that eclipses everything. I really value and I'm quite jealous over the time and my commitment with my family. For some academics, their job is their lifestyle, but that's absolutely not for me; but I can see it encroaching and I'm always trying to hold it back.

Compared to other participants, this woman was under much greater pressure from her extended family to provide care for several generations while pursuing her career. Although she willingly accepted this, she was also enthusiastic about her career, worked long hours on the days that she came to the university, and maintained high levels of scholarly productivity.

Several interviewees also mentioned that elderly parents occupied large amounts of their time and were reasons for making work-related concessions. The female lecturer quoted above, who also had several young children, said, "My mother's terminally ill ... and I'm rostered amongst my own siblings to look after her [on] the weekends." Another woman in a junior position at the teaching university explained how she ended up staying in New Zealand rather than working overseas when her mother became terminally ill: "I was offered a post-doctoral fellowship in [an overseas country], so I was going to go there. It was a great opportunity. But when my mother's [cancer] diagnosis was made, it was a very bad prognosis; I made the decision I was going to maximize the amount of time I could spend with her." Men also talked about ailing parents, and a senior man spoke of the last days of his mother's life: "The more difficult part of my life was when my mother became ill, so it was a matter of trying to adjust the time I could put into looking after her and doing my academic work." However, women were more likely than men to report devoting weeks and even years to these activities and to making major career concessions for the care of frail parents. Generally, making such concessions for family reasons tended to have a number of negative consequences for their careers, especially in the current university environment.

Confidence and the Academic Marketplace

Developing new projects, submitting articles for publication, and applying for funding or promotion all require confidence and sustained belief in one's abilities and scholarship. In the present university milieu, researchers are required to sell their ideas to publishers, granting agencies, promotion committees, and future employers. Studies suggest that males are more likely to believe that their scholarship is worthy, to portray themselves as experts, and to apply for grants or promotion – even when they think it is a long shot (Brooks 1997; Fels 2004; Sax 2008).

Confidence: 1973

Most participants in the 1973 interviews had few expectations of reaching the top of the profession and commented that young girls were generally socialized to think of marriage, family, and domestic security rather than a professional career. For example, a former doctoral student in science said that ambition was "fostered more in boys than in girls. It's easier for girls to get over their ambitious motives and still retain their good self-image ... I know some very intelligent girls who are satisfied doing nothing. Well, I shouldn't say nothing – being housewives" (Baker 1975, 195). Later, the same woman said, "Female graduate students unconsciously absorb the idea that they will have problems, that they won't get to the top, that they will have to compete with men, and that they will have an extra load [housework and childcare]" (ibid., 196). She felt that these social understandings and expectations discouraged women from aspiring to academic careers.

A few interviewees felt comfortable in academia and believed that they could or had become successful in a male-dominated profession. However, as we also saw in previous chapters, many women felt that their male colleagues did not always believe that married women academic had a right to their job and salary, or that academic women were as competent as men. These perceptions tended to anger the female participants and helped to undermine their confidence.

Confidence: 2008

The 2008 study also revealed a lack of academic confidence among many of the women subjects, even some who had already reached the uppermost academic rank. In contrast, the men reported higher levels of ambition and professional confidence, with one mentioning that he had tried for promotion before he was genuinely qualified. This professor, who worked at the research university, spoke about previous applications for promotion that he did not really think he would get: "In some cases, I knew I hadn't published enough to get promoted." When I asked if he had applied anyway, he said, "Yes, yes [*laughing*]."

Several of the male participants seemed to view the promotional procedures or ways of gaining promotion as a game. For instance, another professor at the same university, who was a married father, discussed the circumstances of his final promotion to professor, which had occurred when he worked in the United Kingdom. After I asked if he had expected this promotion earlier in his career, he commented, "No ... Because it never even dawned on me ... I think I did eventually become much more self-conscious and thought gosh, you know, I'm quite an asset to the university and I'm doing all the things that I'm supposed to be doing and I'm being head of department ... I thought, well, this is a game ... I'm clearly performing at a level that one would expect of a professor. So I applied and yeah they recognized that, and I got my promotion."

Another married father, who was a senior lecturer, spoke with assurance: "I can see how I could justify promotion to full professor in three to four years [after the next promotion], based on my books." An associate professor, a married father in his mid-forties, was confident that his final academic promotion would occur soon: "I will certainly have enough publications in a year's time ... and significant ones – to justify a professorship." These remarks made by the men at the research university illustrate their higher degree of optimism about gaining promotion. They also show a stronger acknowledgment that the lifetime record of publications usually forms the basis of promotion to the highest rank, especially in the research universities.

Previous studies have suggested that women's lower confidence is partly influenced by lack of collegial acknowledgment and recognition. As noted earlier, women's research projects often involve smaller qualitative studies, sometimes with feminist perspectives and female collaborators, which tend to receive less acknowledgment and approval from male colleagues (Leahey 2006). Studies also indicate that colleagues give women's publications less credit for promotion, perhaps because they are perceived as less scholarly (Monroe et al. 2008). Consequently, more female academics are nervous about applying for promotion (Probert 2005) and have a less pronounced sense of entitlement (Valian 2004).

Several women in the 2008 interviews openly doubted their intellectual abilities despite winning doctoral scholarships, obtaining PhDs from prominent universities, and finding an academic position in the research university. As we saw in earlier quotes, a single mother who had graduated on scholarship from a reputable overseas university nonetheless thought that she wasn't "clever enough" to be promoted to the professoriate. A senior woman, reminiscing about whether she envisioned becoming a professor when she was younger, made a similar comment: "I don't think I thought I was either clever enough or the right kind of person." When she was encouraged by a colleague to apply for a professorial position in New Zealand, she said, "You've got to be kidding!" Another senior woman talked about her final promotion to professor: "I was encouraged to apply for a chair by [an academic manager]. I would never have dreamt of applying otherwise ... I would have assumed I'd never have got that promotion." When I asked her why she doubted that she would be successful, she downplayed both the quantity and quality of her work, perhaps as her colleagues had done in the past.

Several participants, mostly women, had not applied for promotion for years, believing – some with good reason – that their chances were slim. Others said that they were waiting until they were certain that their application would be successful because they had heard that the standards were very rigorous. Two women doubted that they would ever be professionally successful, attributing their "low self-esteem" to past incidents of emotional or verbal abuse from parents or former male partners. However, many women said that their caring duties reduced their time for additional time-consuming activities such as applying for promotion. One woman from a cultural minority background reported little time to apply because of her caring activities but also doubted her ability to negotiate through an occupational environment that seemed to her "to privilege white middle-class backgrounds."

Half the mothers in the 2008 study struggled as single parents, saying that they had neither the time nor the energy to apply for promotion. Other participants reported that they wanted a "balanced life" and were unable or unwilling to undertake the amount of work they believed was required to reach the professoriate, but this kind of remark was particularly prevalent among mothers with young children. The fact that so many of the women in the 2008 study assumed that they would never reach the senior ranks of academia remains challenging for academic managers and equity officers.

Conclusion

Numerous studies have found that promotion or progression through the ranks of academia are largely influenced by publication rates and secondarily by career longevity (Currie, Thiele, and Harris 2002; Monroe et al. 2008; Nakhaie 2007). Promotion is also mediated by readiness to apply, by self-confidence as a scholar, and by collegial recognition of the value of particular types of research and publications. Although neither the 1973 nor the 2008 interviews contained objective measures of productivity, both gathered material about the perceived impact of gender and parental status on the academic careers of participants.

In both studies, women were much more likely than the males to downplay their intelligence, their research outputs, and the worthiness of their scholarship, and many more of them implied that they felt like outsiders in their own profession. In the 1973 interviews, most participants displayed low expectations of academic promotion, claiming that women had to be twice as productive as men to gain comparable promotion and some reporting various incidents of sex discrimination. One example was that women's voices were less often heard by both colleagues and students.

In the 2008 interviews, the men expressed much more confidence than the women in their professional abilities and chances of future success, sometimes viewing promotion as a game they knew they could win. In contrast, the women were much more likely to suggest that they would never reach the top of the hierarchy. More importantly, many also said that they did not *want* to do so and mentioned negative consequences of becoming a senior professor, such as loss of friendships and other interests, long hours, and too much responsibility.

In the interviews, the women projected lower levels of entitlement to promotion than the men, which probably reflected their perceived treatment from male colleagues and managers. Many seemed reluctant to admit their own career ambition or to express pride in their research and publications, perhaps because they felt that doing so was unfeminine or socially unacceptable. However, their comments also showed lower levels of confidence and self-esteem than the men's, yet participants of both sexes believed they worked hard and deserved more institutional recognition. The higher level of work-related confidence among males has been found in other studies of academics (Aisenberg and Harrington 1988; Gerdes 2006; Probert 2005) but also among other professional and management workers (Kreitner 2009; Moore 1988).

Although academics do not work nine-to-five, their research and publishing projects tend to follow them home, and expectations of research productivity have increased in recent decades in all the liberal states. In the 2008 study, more women than men felt that they could not devote the requisite hours to merit promotion and consequently tailored their career expectations accordingly. In addition, they often questioned the fairness of academic practices, including the priorities inherent in the promotional system. They also demonstrated less knowledge of academic practices. At the same time, more women talked about their family life as of central importance to them.

For promotion to the highest rank, universities have always rewarded academics who work long hours, publish widely, and bring prestige.

They also value scholars who feel comfortable in the university environment, are respected by their colleagues, remain committed to their discipline, and are employed full-time throughout their working lives. These priorities have remained relatively unchanged over the decades, despite the development of equity initiatives and family-friendly policies. Academics who are unable or unwilling to play by these rules of the game will inevitably fall behind. In the two sets of interviews, this included a disproportionate number of women, especially those who were mothers.

Explaining the Academic Gender Gap

7

Interviewer: Do you think that your gender has influenced your career in any way?

Male professor, New Zealand, 2008: No, I don't think so. I can't recall anything that was gender specific.

I suppose my gender might not have [had any impact on my career] if I had decided not to have children. I think that's the way it impacted most.

– FEMALE ASSOCIATE PROFESSOR, NEW ZEALAND, 2008

Postsecondary Education and Work-Related Practices

Currently, more employed women reach professional and managerial positions than they did in the 1970s, reflecting women's higher educational attainment and occupational expectations (OECD 2008b; Pettit and Hook 2009). Increased levels of female employment may also demonstrate the positive impact of the equity and family-friendly policies generated by governments, employers, and unions during the past four decades. Rising levels of maternal employment also result from economic pressures. More households now require two incomes to make ends meet than they did in the mid-twentieth century, as material aspirations have intensified and living costs have risen relative to male wages (OECD 2007a, 2008b).

Rates of separation and divorce have also grown since the late 1960s, and more women now live in households without a male earner and therefore need to support themselves and their children (Bradbury and Norris 2005). Increasingly, the governments of the liberal states are tightening the eligibility rules for income support and requiring more able-bodied adults to work their way out of poverty. This includes single mothers, who still have the lowest household incomes but had greater access to income support in the 1970s (Baker 2006; Lunt 2008; MacDonald 2009).

Despite the increases in women's education, employment rates, and earnings, work patterns still vary statistically by sex in all the liberal states, which is also visible in academia. For example, males and females still specialize in somewhat different educational fields, with conse-quences for employment opportunities and future salaries. Male doctor-ates are still more likely than their female counterparts to pursue full-time academic careers that begin in their twenties and remain un-interrupted until retirement. Statistically, women are more likely than men to take employment leave, usually for caring activities, even when they attain the highest educational qualifications and develop profes-sional careers (Acker and Webber 2006; Berberet et al. 2005; Tizard and Owen 2001).

The research discussed in previous chapters has shown that despite the pushes and pulls to enter the labour force, women in all the liberal states tend to retain a weaker attachment than men to paid work. Despite rising qualifications, fewer women than men reach the top of their chosen profession or accept senior positions requiring long working hours; more believe that managerial positions will bring negative per-sonal consequences, such as overwork and the loss of friends (Baker 2010a; Fels 2004; Monroe et al. 2008; Probert 2005). Even when women obtain PhDs and tenured academic jobs, their achievements are less likely to be recognized by colleagues, and they tend to receive less social support for both careers and domestic responsibilities than men. Social pressures to provide care and maintain work-life balance, combined with less support for career development, help to explain why women are more likely than men to make employment concessions for family. These concessions include working part-time while their children are young, finding new jobs when husbands choose to relocate, and retiring at the same time as their older partners but earlier than their male colleagues.

Although this book focuses on occupational achievements and academic success, we cannot lose sight of the fact that pursuits other than paid work can lead to fulfilling lives. These may include creative and leisure activities, voluntary community service, the development of friendships, providing care for children and the frail elderly, and creating a safe and satisfying home life for all family members. Such activities seldom lead to wealth or prestige but provide satisfaction, happiness, and well-functioning homes and communities.

Although paid and unpaid work has gradually become less gendered over the past forty years, many families and communities continue to give priority to male careers and earning potential. When employed women become parents, they often experience a motherhood penalty in terms of rank and average earnings, partly because they are expected to assume the care work. Academic practices place considerable value on peer review and recommendations by senior colleagues, but women's research is sometimes seen as less scholarly or theoretically relevant than that of men. This is especially the case for research based on feminist theories, that interviews women or children, and that adopts a qualitative approach.

Academic Work and University Restructuring

In Chapter 3, I argued that many public universities in the liberal states have engaged in neo-liberal practices such as increasing their emphasis on cost cutting, administrative reporting, and inter-university benchmarking. More than in the 1970s, university administrators spend more time searching for private donations and trying to raise their institution's profile – both nationally and internationally – through publicity and marketing activities. This kind of restructuring has taken place in response to broader economic changes, including rising student enrolments and higher operating costs, smaller state grants relative to university expenditures, and stronger international competition for students and their accompanying tuition fees and state grants. The academic profession itself has become more competitive as many universities raise entry qualifications for full-time jobs and expect greater levels of research productivity for tenure and promotion. More scholars now move across national borders to seek employment and promotion, enlarging the pool of applicants but also increasing the competition for local candidates.

The academic profession has changed in a variety of ways over the decades. New technology, including Powerpoint, has changed the nature of lecturing, and e-mail and the Internet have made certain aspects of the job easier and faster. However, technology is constantly changing, requiring continual relearning. With this new technology and administrative restructuring, academics have been forced to accept more responsibility for some tasks formerly done by administrative staff, such as retrieving work-related material from the Internet, printing agendas and documentation for committee meetings, and typing their own article and book manuscripts. In addition, they are now expected to deal with students from a more diverse range of socioeconomic and cultural backgrounds, including more women, foreign students, and those with greater obligations to family and employers. In some universities, more of the institutional decisions are now made by professional managers, although scholars still participate in decision making relating to hiring, tenure, and promotion. All these developments affect both men and women, but studies suggest that female academics tend to embrace new administrative requirements, undergraduate teaching, and student mentoring with more enthusiasm or stronger feelings of responsibility than their male colleagues do (Bernard 1964; Brooks 1997; Glazer-Raymo 1999; Jacobs 2004; Monroe et al. 2008).

In some jurisdictions, new reporting requirements heighten the workload for both administrators and academics, including annual performance reviews, more rigorous ethics reviews for empirical research, and national research assessment exercises. Universities are also creating written guidelines for working conditions and performance expectations, often through negotiations with professional associations and unions. For example, the research university in the 2008 New

Zealand study now expects academics to allocate 40 percent of their time to teaching, 40 percent to research, and 20 percent to service or administration. In this university, teaching comprises less than half of the normal workload, and academics are expected to allocate equal time to research.[1] These workload models may seem somewhat arbitrary and often differ substantially from actual workloads, but they can be used as tools of regulation and surveillance (Malcolm and Zukas 2009). However, department chairs or heads typically retain greater control over teaching schedules than research activities. Lectures and committee meetings are set at specific dates, and academics are required to meet these timetables, but time-poor academics could more feasibly postpone or spend less time on their research and publications.

Tenured or permanent academics typically enjoy considerable personal control over research activities, including their choice of topics, research partners, methodology, project duration, and dissemination of their findings. Most academics are still permitted to choose which conferences to attend and where they submit their articles for publication consideration. However, universities with heightened requirements for performance have added a greater level of surveillance and monitoring to research activities and types of outputs.

Clearly, levels of managerialism vary considerably by jurisdiction and institution. When university managers and administrators (such as senior management teams or human resources departments) gain more control over decision making, they sometimes introduce new reporting mechanisms to enhance efficiency and raise productivity. However, equity advocates, feminists, and academic unions have also pressed for written guidelines on workload expectations and promotion criteria to ensure fairness and prevent the old boys' network from making biased or preferential decisions. Even when unions object to new reporting requirements, they are sometimes powerless to prevent their implementation, especially in universities with voluntary membership or a small percentage of academics who are union members. As hiring becomes more competitive and universities increase levels of bureaucracy, higher standards of productivity and heightened reporting requirements become normalized, especially for young academics.

Developing or enhancing the two-tier hiring system has been one way in which managers have attempted to increase the research productivity of tenured or permanent academics. A growing percentage of teachers and researchers are now hired on short-term contracts to teach large undergraduate courses, to serve as teaching or research assistants, to work in research centres, and to help manage externally funded projects. Many well-qualified women benefit from these short-term jobs, especially mothers with young children, but they do not always lead to promotional careers, rising salaries with seniority, or substantial collegial recognition.

In contrast, tenured academics and especially senior research chairs are expected to attract external research funds as well as new research collaborators and postgraduate students, and to bring prestige to the university through these endeavours. Some managers have also enhanced the economic value of research by retaining larger portions of the external research grants gained by academics as overheads to contribute to operating costs. In addition, governments in several liberal states (Australia, New Zealand, and the United Kingdom) have tried to encourage universities to boost their research productivity by rewarding them financially for their performance through national research assessment exercises. What impact have these changes had on the academic gender gap?

Focusing on Research and Internationalization: Gendered Consequences
One of the most noticeable gendered consequences of university restructuring relates to the increased emphasis on research productivity, international competitiveness, and institutional reputation. First, the strengthened focus on research tends to shift the workload balance among the three strands of teaching, research, and service by providing additional rewards for the entrepreneurial research activities that are more often prioritized by male academics. Women continue to be hired in larger numbers in teaching universities and in departments that value the pastoral care of students, where they tend to devote more time to teaching and service. Perhaps as a consequence, they produce fewer peer-reviewed publications than men, but publications are typically

valued more than teaching in academic promotion, especially in the research universities (Bellas and Toutkoushian 1999; Monroe et al. 2008; Nakhaie 2002, 2007).

Second, the university preference for external research funding tends to be gendered because granting agencies and other external funders often favour large-scale projects with multiple collaborators using quantitative research methods. These projects are typically led by senior men (Leahey 2006; Mohrman, Ma, and Baker 2008). When women focus on qualitative research, and particularly when they choose feminist or qualitative projects, they are less likely to be awarded external research grants, but they are also less likely to apply for such grants (Probert 2005; Waisbren et al. 2008). With fewer resources for research assistants, travel, and project dissemination, they may need to work harder, projecting unfavourable role models for younger female academics.

Third, the new emphasis on research competition and entrepreneurialism requires academics to justify and defend their project goals and scholarship, and to seek new publishing venues in a competitive environment. Being published in high-prestige journals and with scholarly book publishers has become more challenging as academics experience greater pressure to publish. They may receive numerous rejections before they see their work in print and must continually justify their scholarly decisions. This aspect of their work requires high levels of personal and intellectual confidence, which are more often found in men than in women (Probert 2005; Sax 2008).

Fourth, the focus on research and publishing exacerbates the long-hours culture and intensifies work-related stress levels, with gendered implications. Academics are increasingly made to feel that they are never doing enough and should be working longer hours to initiate new projects. They are also pressured to gain more and larger grants to support their research, to financially assist the institution through grant overheads, and to provide more opportunities for their graduate students to develop their capabilities. Researchers are also expected to publish in "world class" journals, which typically have higher rejection rates and require more revisions (Kinman and Jones 2004). Universities seldom expect academics to do all their research on campus, unless they work in laboratories or on team projects. However, research activities can easily expand into weekends, evenings, and holidays. This is particularly challenging for those who value work-life balance and for parents with young children (more often women).

Fifth, the growing focus on international prestige sometimes requires academics to generate research networks with colleagues in other jurisdictions, to travel to distant conferences, to take their sabbatical leave at other universities (including in foreign countries), and to apply for international funding for research projects. Especially in Australia and New Zealand, travelling to international conferences means time-consuming and costly overseas trips. Travel can be especially difficult for individuals with children or frail parents. Furthermore, these international activities require time, money, extensive professional networks, and a certain level of instrumental social capital, which women are less likely to develop than men (van Emmerik 2006).

In heterosexual couples, the man's salary often provides the majority of household income. Academic men typically earn more than their partners, many of whom provide valuable unpaid services for the entire household. Academic women's lower marriage rates and domestic support from partners, combined with their smaller earnings, leave them less time and money for professional activities. More discretionary money could enable academics to join professional associations, subscribe to scholarly journals, attend international conferences, or spend sabbatical leave in other jurisdictions, all of which would contribute to their social capital by enabling them to increase their publications and national/international reputations.

Gender as a Career Constraint for Women

Careers can be enhanced or constrained by goals and ambitions that children are encouraged to develop at home and at school, as well as by the way in which adults are treated by colleagues and managers in the workplace. Males tend to be given greater encouragement than females to plan for lifelong employment, to aspire to professional careers, and to aim for the top of their chosen profession (Butler 1990; Connell 2000). Many participants in the 1973 study claimed that they were socialized to become wives and mothers, attentive educators, and accommodating service providers but not creators and disseminators of knowledge. The older women in both studies most commonly mentioned gendered expectations from parents who thought they should be getting married or having babies rather than developing academic careers. The 1973 interviewees contravened gendered expectations simply by becoming academics. Both male and female participants in the two studies mentioned that their father provided more encouragement than their mother for their career ambitions.

Most male participants in the 2008 study were baffled by the question about the influence of gender on their career and could not answer it. Several told anecdotes about career problems experienced by their academic wives, but most perceived gender as a female issue that was not related to them, and though more male than female participants saw themselves as experts, international scholars, or future academic leaders, they did not associate this professional confidence with gender socialization.

In contrast, women in both sets of interviews spoke at length about gender discrimination in the workplace, lack of respect for female voices from students and colleagues, social exclusion from collegial networks, and especially the lack of institutional support for the maternity and childrearing issues that challenged their career advancement. In the 1973 study, the interviewees reported that their male colleagues viewed them as less capable and less committed to the profession than men and that they also assumed that the women did not *need* university jobs, because they were married to a male earner. These women also mentioned less respect for women's scholarly achievements from parents, partners, colleagues, and students. In the 2008 study, most women believed that motherhood was a more significant career barrier than gender, and both mothers and childless women mentioned the career-related challenges of combining motherhood with academic work. They also suggested that mothers were treated differently than fathers, both in the workplace and at home, reporting that parents, partners, and children expected mothers to make employment sacrifices, especially for children. In contrast, they stated that family members more often acknowledged and supported the work-related responsibilities of fathers.

Although the academic salaries of women are rising relative to those of men, women continue to earn lower salaries, largely influenced by their employment characteristics (Bernard 1964; Brooks 1997; Monroe et al. 2008). For example, compared to men, female academics tend to be younger, more recently hired, grouped in the lower ranks, and less likely to work full-time in research universities for their entire employment lives. In addition, academic men are more likely to work in the more prestigious universities and in disciplines with higher salaries, such as business, science, engineering, and medicine (Auriol 2007). Some of these factors reflect personal or family choices, although these are always shaped by social and cultural circumstances.

Work-Related Choices

Investigating agency can be challenging because personal choices are often implicit or unacknowledged by study participants and are sometimes presented as structural constraints. In other words, participants may make contradictory statements about which activities are based on their own agency or choices, and which they perceive to be imposed upon them by circumstances. Even individuals of the same sex who are working at the same rank in the same occupation tend to perceive that they have differing options, obligations, and responsibilities, both at work and at home.

Researchers, however, have found patterns in the reporting and perceptions of choices relating to earning and caring, suggesting that these are moulded by socio-cultural and class-based ideas about gender-appropriate behaviour and good parenting. Clearly, career-related decisions are made within a socioeconomic context and are influenced by perceived costs, benefits, and consequences. They are also shaped by social support and the decisions of others, particularly partners and children but also extended families, communities, potential employers, and governments.

This book has shown that males and females tend to make different choices about the academic disciplines or sub-disciplines they study, how long they remain in university, and the type of work they value after graduation. However, these choices have changed over the decades. For example, in the liberal states, few women in the 1960s and '70s continued their education to the doctoral level or pursued full-time academic careers after motherhood (Baker 1975; Bernard 1964; Epstein 1971). Since then, ideas about the value of education and employment have become less gendered, and more women now expect to graduate from university, earn their own living, and contribute to society through paid work.

More women are also deciding to enter academic disciplines previously dominated by men and to complete a PhD. However, most female doctoral students continue to specialize in the humanities, education, and the social sciences, whereas engineering and the physical sciences remain customary choices for men (Auriol 2007, 2010). Parents, advisors, and students themselves view certain areas of specialization as more appropriate for either women or men. Work cultures also vary by discipline, making it easier or more difficult for scholars to flourish in particular departments based on their sex, parental status, and personal values.

Unfortunately, material consequences follow the disciplinary decisions that men and women make, as men's choices typically lead to higher levels of employment and larger salaries (Statistics Canada 2009). Women are more likely than men to study subjects in which they are interested or that lead to service-related jobs that can be combined with childrearing; by contrast, men gravitate to subjects that lead to lucrative or high-status careers (Auriol 2007; Boreham et al. 2008; Brooks 1997). Increasingly, however, both male and female students are influenced by prevailing opportunities for employment and financial reward.

The research discussed throughout this book suggests that more male than female PhDs report that career success is important to their self-esteem and future. Men more often admit that they *want* to reach the top of their profession and actively seek out mentors and other instrumental relationships to help them learn the rules of the game and win timely promotion (Burris 2004; Lim and Herrer-Sobek 2000; Monroe et al. 2008). Men tend to search for full-time positions in high-profile research universities, which provide them with opportunities to carry out funded research, gain scholarly publications, and attain high salaries and esteem from their peers.

Conversely, women doctorates express more ambivalence about striving for high-pressure careers and sometimes accept jobs that pay less but are located closer to parents, partners, and friends or that better enable them to manage care work (Comer and Stites-Doe 2006; Probert 2005; Sax 2008). Because working full-time and being promoted through the ranks require long hours and measurable indicators of research productivity, female PhDs with infants or toddlers may initially accept temporary and part-time positions to help them manage their domestic workload. Others choose employment in teaching universities with less publishing pressure in order to accommodate childrearing without undue stress (Bassett 2005). Still others accept non-academic positions with regular business hours, such as jobs in research centres or the public service, in an attempt to contain their working hours.

Generally, more academic mothers than fathers report that they are satisfied to teach long-term on a part-time or contractual basis or at a lower-ranking or local institution. However, this "preference" is often based on the assumption that mothers should or are required by circumstances to take responsibility for most of the domestic and care work. Some academic women erroneously believe that they can easily upgrade to a full-time job or a more distinguished university when their children enter school and their care obligations subside. However, selecting a workplace is not always simply a matter of personal choice, as we have seen throughout this book.

Most academics value the autonomy to pursue their own research topics, but men seem more jealously to guard their time for research and writing (Brooks 1997; Monroe et al. 2008). They are also more likely to view themselves as specialists, experts, and men of knowledge who are pushing back the intellectual frontiers with their important theoretical contributions. In contrast, academic women are more likely to verbally downplay the value of their scholarly work and professional experience, both with colleagues and in interviews, and to show more diffidence in their presentation of self on websites and in curricula vitae (Goffman 1959; Menzies and Newson 2008; Probert 2005). This could be considered an example of performing gender or showing appropriate modesty, but displays of expertise and intellectual confidence often influence the perceptions of colleagues and managers. Furthermore, an assured presentation of self has become even more significant in the competitive environment of the restructuring university.

Studies have found that female scholars continue to allocate more time than men to teaching preparation, student meetings, and service to the university, community, and extended family (Acker and Feuerverger 1996; Bird, Litt, and Wang 2004). In my 2008 study, the female participants expressed more social responsibility about service-related jobs in the department and criticized male colleagues who avoided university service work but posed as "big men on campus" or sought-after international consultants. However, some clearly experienced difficulty in saying no to requests for assistance from managers, students, and family members, even when this interfered with their academic duties and promotional opportunities.

In the New Zealand interviews, some women seemed less aware than the men of the unwritten rules governing the academic marketplace, whereas other women seemed to believe that they could change the rules or ignore them without undue consequences. Both sets of interviews as well as the broader research suggest that academic women have been less interested in playing the promotional game, believing that senior positions imply negative consequences such as loss of friends, overly long working hours, or taking on onerous responsibilities. Furthermore, more women than men in my 2008 interviews mentioned that they disapproved of colleagues who engaged in self-promotion or appeared too eager to seek career advancement. There was some suggestion in both sets of interviews and the research that women who try to progress through the ranks are viewed more harshly than men and seen as scheming, ruthless, and even as honorary men. Many female scholars but only a few men in the 2008 study reported that they gained more satisfaction and tangible rewards from contact with students, classroom teaching, preparing widely read introductory textbooks, and assisting with administration than from activities oriented to research leadership or international scholarship.

As universities pressure academics to publish or perish, gaining publication acceptance by scholarly presses and high-impact journals becomes more challenging. First, with globalizing markets, many publishing companies are experiencing increased competition, are becoming more conscious of the bottom line, and are therefore more selective in their ventures. Second, as universities emphasize the importance of publication, scholarly journals and publishers receive more manuscripts to review. Third, submitting manuscripts to journals and publishing companies opens one's work to criticism, and assertions of expertise are often accompanied by conflict and controversy. Typically, women have been encouraged to avoid or attempt to resolve conflict (Bernard 1964; Brooks 1997; Monroe et al. 2008).

Despite these patterns, more women are choosing to gain doctorates, to work as academics, and to apply for grants and promotion, and more are reaching the highest ranks of academia. As earlier chapters show, the percentage of women in senior academic positions has grown in the liberal states from about 5 percent in the 1970s to about 20 percent now. Furthermore, more senior academic women are choosing to move into managerial positions (such as department head, dean, president, and vice-chancellor), and some of these are currently serving as role models for younger scholars. With new equity obligations and a larger percentage of women in high-ranking positions, women's contributions to the university are more often valued by both managers and colleagues.

At the same time, academic women continue to retire earlier than academic men and are more likely to accept part-time work as a form of gradual retirement (Berberet et al. 2005; Tizard and Owen 2001). Reasons for this may relate to reduced job satisfaction, which has been associated with lower academic rank at the time of retirement. More women complete their PhDs at older ages after working in other jobs and/or raising children at home, and only a minority are promoted beyond the intermediate ranks and/or gain the same level of collegial recognition as their male colleagues do before retirement. Tizard and Owen (2001) found that high-ranking British academics (usually male) tend to retire later, partly because high remuneration and status are difficult to relinquish. In the past, some jurisdictions, such as the United Kingdom, had an earlier expected retirement age for women, although few now retain mandatory retirement or male-female variations in the retirement age.

Women retire at a slightly younger average age than their male colleagues, as many partnered women coincide the timing of their retirement with that of their husband, who is usually older (Statistics Canada 2008). In addition, female academics on the brink of retirement often report that they want to spend more time in leisure activities or with their grandchildren, who increasingly live in another location. After retirement from the university, more academic men continue some form of paid work for a longer period, such as consulting in fields relating to their expertise, whereas women tend to curb their paid work earlier (Tizard and Owen 2001).

Some of these gendered patterns are influenced by social expectations, family relationships and support, access to institutional rewards, and social capital, whereas others are shaped by desire for work-life balance. Women's typical work patterns may lead to lower ranks and salaries, but they also provide more varied personal lives with stronger social and family networks.

Family and Gender Relations: Social Changes and Enduring Patterns

Since the 1970s, a number of socio-demographic trends have influenced family and gender relations, encouraging more women to become self-supporting and to value economic autonomy. Educational levels have increased, especially for women, cohabitation rates have risen, couples are marrying later and having fewer children, more relationships are ending in separation, and living costs have increased relative to male wages (Baker 2010b, 2010d). With better educational qualifications and job experience, more women can now support themselves and their children outside of legal marriage, though single mothers struggle to combine earning and caring (Edin and Lein 1997; Walter 2002).

In the 1973 interviews, some participants felt that both marriage and children interfered with a full-time academic career. During that era, it was not uncommon for husbands to try to limit their wife's employment by insisting that she had no need to work and/or expecting her to take responsibility for all the domestic tasks even if she worked full-time. Several wives reported divorcing partners who would not support their career or share the household chores. Although the grounds for divorce in Canada during the 1960s and early 1970s were quite restrictive and the process itself was expensive, divorce was easier in the United States, where some of the participants originated.

Many of the mothers in the 1973 study mentioned that they did not work for pay when their children were young, as there were few public childcare services at that time and childrearing was viewed as a maternal career. Consequently, these mothers cared for their children at home for years before completing a doctorate or returning to full-time academic work, but this period outside the labour force often curtailed their academic careers. Fewer mothers in the 2008 interviews cared for their children at home, but parenting standards had become more intensive, as I discussed in Chapter 2 (Hays 1996; Hochschild 1997; Wall 2009). Parents are now expected to spend more time and attention supervising and instructing their children despite the heightened economic need and personal desire for two household incomes. In addition, women are still more likely than men to shoulder the responsibility for childcare and indoor chores, even though they do less household work than a generation ago.

Childcare facilities are now available on many university campuses, and more fathers share childcare and domestic chores (Baxter, Hewitt, and Haynes 2008; Ranson 2009). Nevertheless, childcare services remain difficult to access outside regular business hours and are often unavailable for sick children, suggesting that many parents continue to experience childcare dilemmas that interfere with full-time employment (Baker 2011b). In the 2008 interviews, the women were much more likely than the men to report childcare problems because more women were parenting alone, and many families still viewed the mother as the main care provider.

Both sets of interviews included successful academic women who were well regarded by their colleagues and highly productive in terms of research and publications. However, the studies also included women who reported that a balanced life was more important to them than occupational success. In the 2008 study, this kind of comment was more likely to be made by mothers who worked at the teaching university and whose children were young. Research suggests that employment differences that appear to be influenced by gender are more accurately attributable to motherhood. This indicates that cultural definitions of good mothering encourage mothers – but not fathers – to make employment sacrifices for their children. A growing body of research refers to the motherhood penalty, which reveals much lower earnings and job status for employed mothers than for childless women (Baker 2010d; Zhang 2009).

Marriage, Housework, and Childcare Constraints

Because more female than male academics remain single, are separated or divorced, and are parenting alone, more of them retain sole responsibility for childcare, household work, and home maintenance. Many must pay all the bills and do the domestic tasks, and are less likely to have another adult in the household to celebrate their academic achievements, help proofread their scholarly papers, and listen to their work-related or domestic concerns. With lower average salaries and household incomes than men, many female academics feel that they cannot afford to hire home cleaners or extensive childcare services. Especially for single parents, the responsibility for the daily care and supervision of young children tends to reduce time and energy for research and writing, or time for leisure and sleep (Acker and Armenti 2004; Baker 2010d; Bassett 2005).

Living arrangements can create large differentials in income and professional opportunities among female academics, as well as between men and women. The single and childless women in both sets of interviews typically viewed their marital and parental status as career advantages but not always as social advantages. With fewer family responsibilities than married mothers, they could more easily work in the evenings or weekends, travel to conferences, and take sabbatical leave in distant places. Academic women with male partners, especially men with prestigious jobs, typically enjoy higher household incomes than unattached women and often gain additional social capital from their partner's networks.

When academics live with heterosexual partners, however, they tend *not* to share the household work equally (Baxter, Hewitt, and Haynes 2008; Ranson 2009).[2] Most participants in the 2008 study reported an unequal and gendered division of labour, even when women worked full-time and their male partners were retired or semi-retired. Both men and women also stated that women maintained higher standards of housekeeping, and several men expressed annoyance that their female partner expected them to do more cleaning or to do it according to her (higher) standards. All the partnered women in the New Zealand study said that they did a disproportionate amount of housework, sometimes to get the job done properly. In many of these families, contentious gendered differences were apparent about the importance of housework, when and how it should be done, and the division of specific tasks between partners. When jobs were not done, or not done "properly," women often took over.

From childhood, girls are still mentored to take housework and childcare seriously and are often expected to help their mothers around the home. After marriage, women typically lack the necessary bargaining power to insist that their husband does his fair share, although what is fair is often contested (Bittman and Pixley 1997; Mason and Goulden 2004; Ranson 2009). For example, many male partners in the 2008 study felt that they did more housework than other men, and more than their partner gave them credit for. However, some male participants clearly felt that their breadwinner status or larger household earnings exempted them from indoor domestic chores.

These findings show that women's employment strategies are often influenced by other people's choices and constraints, including their partner's working hours, his willingness to share domestic tasks, the needs of their children and aging parents, and the availability of childcare and paid work in the community. Regardless of their educational qualifications or occupational prestige, the work-related concessions that women tend to make for motherhood and marriage generally limit their promotion through the ranks (Baker 2010d; Zhang 2009).

Family-Related Choices

This book shows that academic men and women in the liberal states continue to make differing choices about partnering and parenting. The social research finds that most adults expect to live with intimate partners, to become parents, and to integrate parenthood with their careers, and in these respects academics are no exception (Bracken, Allen, and Dean 2006; VIF 2008; Weston et al. 2004). In accordance with wider demographic patterns, academics now marry at older ages than they did in the early 1970s. Highly educated men are more likely than comparable women to marry or to cohabit, and most continue to choose slightly younger and less educated partners who have less prestigious jobs, work shorter hours, and earn less money (Baker 2010b; Beaujot 2000; Creamer 2006). These patterns tend to give men more social capital. For example, a male doctorate working full-time and earning more money than his female partner typically enjoys more opportunities to prioritize his career ambitions. If partnered men separate, they are more likely than women to re-partner and to do so faster (Baker 2010b).

Although these trends may be a male choice over which a female partner has little control, many women are nevertheless attracted to older successful men who earn high salaries and are professionally confident and senior ranking. In addition, many willingly make employment concessions for their partners, which they justify for love, companionship, and the desire for children, as well as an opportunity to enjoy more interesting lifestyles or higher living standards. This means that some educated wives continue to be grateful for any employment they can find if it permits them to work in their profession and retain their marriage. Partnered women sometimes accept jobs that their male colleagues would define as inferior. However, many women in the liberal states now seem to have a stronger sense of entitlement to employment equity with men than women had in the 1970s.

Women who pursue full-time academic careers continue to have a higher probability of separation and divorce than their male counterparts. This can be explained partly by their high earning capacity and their financial ability to leave unsatisfying relationships while continuing to pay the bills. Like men, academic women value personal autonomy and want to retain their hard-earned career; if that career appears to be jeopardized by marriage, they can become self-supporting if they choose. However, when academics separate, men have a greater probability of finding a new partner because the marriage market still favours mature professional men with high earnings (Baker 2010c). Women's choices after separation and divorce may be to live alone or as a single parent, or to search long and hard for a partner who is willing to support their career and share the household work. Clearly, many women do find new relationships that are supportive and satisfying.

Academics still tend to delay childbearing until they complete their doctorate, find a permanent or tenure-track job, and obtain tenure, but this often coincides with women's most fertile years and is not always possible (Armenti 2004). Some tenure-stream women choose to remain child-free, whereas others delay childbearing until it is too late. Even when female academics *want* to have a child or more children, a suitable father may not be available or they may worry about the impact of (additional) children on their career. These patterns are typical for women with high levels of education and earning potential (Hagestad and Call 2007), and they help to explain the low marriage and fertility rates of tenure-track women.

Academic women are far more likely than academic men to agonize about the implications of childbearing or childrearing for their career progression. When they do reproduce, they tend to provide the lion's share of the daily care and emotional support for their children, and more women than men become single parents. Childbearing is increasingly seen as a choice, but becoming a single parent seldom is, although most women want to live with their children after separation. These patterns show that family circumstances are influenced by choices but also by a variety of social constraints. These include opportunities to find a suitable partner, the partner's desire to become a parent, the level of his emotional and practical support, the financial implications of parenting, the availability of employment leave and childcare services, and the potential career implications of taking parental leave.

Academic women who become mothers are more likely than academic fathers to believe that they need to "be there" physically to care for their children. Prevalent ideas of good fathering tend to incorporate more delegation of care and focus instead on earning a living and providing back-up childcare (Connell 1995; Wall 2009). Therefore, male academics can choose to be good fathers by working hard at their research and publications, which would enable them to attain promotion, increase their earnings, and support the family at a higher income level. They would still be viewed as good fathers if they performed some childcare in the evenings and weekends. In contrast, many employed mothers feel guilty when they leave their young children in the care of *anyone else* during the day, including well-trained childcare professionals, the children's grandparents, or father. Good mothering is often socially defined as providing daily emotional and hands-on care (Craig 2006; Hays 1996; McMahon 1999).

Women tend to give greater priority than men to household tasks, viewing a clean and tidy home as essential for their own peace of mind and their family's well-being (Baxter, Hewitt, and Haynes 2008; Ranson 2009). Obviously, meals need to be cooked and laundry needs to be done, but these tasks could be performed by partners, children, or hired help. In the 2008 study, many women participants but few men mentioned doing large amounts of housework in the evenings and weekends. When asked why they did not hire domestic help, some seemed to feel that they would be shirking their (female) responsibilities. Others felt unable to afford the cost of cleaning services, whereas some were either ideologically opposed to hiring women to do their "dirty work" or chose to retain control over this domain.

Participants in this study also reported that they were less likely to contract out portions of the *indoor* domestic work than outdoor chores such as gardening, grass cutting, and repairs, which are typically seen as men's work. This suggests that at least this sample of academic men are choosing to relinquish some of the traditional tasks associated with masculinity, possibly to focus more on their scholarly work or gain more leisure time. However, more of the female interviewees retained the traditional gender-related tasks that could reduce their university work time, energy, and career commitment. This form of "doing gender" could be viewed as a type of unconscious compensation for entering a masculine occupation.

Perceptions of family-related responsibilities are partially influenced by women's choice of partners, who are often older men with successful careers and higher salaries, and the high value women typically place on a well-run household. Both of these are moulded by prevalent ideas about gender. In the 2008 study, some participants' constraints seemed to be at least partially self-imposed, such as choosing to do their own housework when hired help was available and affordable, or volunteering to do additional community or family work rather than spending more time on research and publications. These activities also coincide with socially constructed ideas of femininity, especially in New Zealand.

Research suggests that perceptions of responsibilities are influenced by upbringing, social and cultural expectations, household income, time management, and support from partners, parents, and friends. Some female participants in both sets of interviews chose not to rock the boat regarding the unequal division of domestic chores because they felt they lacked the power to change it and did not want to jeopardize their marriage. However, other women managed enormous amounts of care work while maintaining successful academic careers.

Conclusion

The central concern of this book has been to explain the perpetuation of the academic gender gap in the liberal states but also to assess the balance between structural career constraints and the subjectivities or personal preferences and choices of academics. Throughout the previous chapters, I have investigated both behavioural and institutional patterns as well as the subjective perceptions of university-based scholars. My conclusions have been based on national and international statistics, and research from Australia, Canada, New Zealand, the United Kingdom, and the United States. I have also introduced two sets of my own qualitative interviews, one with female academics working in Canada in 1973 and one with male and female scholars working in two types of New Zealand universities in 2008. Verbatim comments from these participants helped to illustrate findings and the research trends in the wider literature. These combined types of data show the extent of change over the decades but also some persistent academic priorities and gendered patterns in work and family life.

The book suggests that hard-working academics with PhDs from top universities who devote long hours to their academic career, publish widely in prestigious scholarly venues, bring esteem to their institution, and work full-time until retirement have always been most highly rewarded by universities (Bernard 1964; Caplow and McGee 1958; Jencks and Riesman 1977). In the past, some of these priorities have discouraged women from embarking on academic careers and have inhibited their progression through the ranks. Fewer women developed full-time academic careers in the 1970s, as they were expected to marry, reproduce, and care for their children at home. When they contravened these gendered expectations and became career-oriented academics, many remained unmarried or childless, and fewer married mothers reached the top of the professional hierarchy.

In recent decades, universities have hired more female scholars and encouraged them to apply for promotion. University managers, professional associations, academic unions, and individuals have established a series of initiatives to assist women employees, including employment equity programs, status of women committees, sexual harassment policies, paid parental leave, campus childcare services, work-life balance initiatives, and special women's mentoring programs. These measures, however, have seldom received either strong financial backing from the university or been the priority of senior managers (Bird, Litt, and Wang 2004). Furthermore, male academics have less often used equity and work-life balance initiatives for fear of stigmatization in a competitive university environment. Consequently, these programs have been seen as most relevant for women (Kinman and Jones 2004).

At the same time, universities have given priority to other strategic goals. In recent decades, managers and administrators have devoted more time and effort to marketing and maintaining or raising institutional prestige in order to gain additional funding and to compete nationally and internationally. They have also embraced expensive new technology for teaching and research. In addition, universities have provided new academic programs for the growing number of students, accommodated students with more diverse backgrounds, and enhanced learning outcomes and student completions. In some jurisdictions, administrative procedures have been strengthened to meet new accountability requirements from the state or to help cope with rising operating costs of universities.

In dealing with these strategic priorities, which relate largely to finances and policy changes, many universities have reinforced their commitment to some of the very practices that contribute to the academic gender gap. With incentives from research assessment exercises, they have strengthened their focus on peer-reviewed publications in high-status publishing venues, an arena in which men have more often excelled. They have hired more senior research stars, most of whom are male, while leaving more of the undergraduate teaching and distance education courses to temporary lecturers who are disproportionately doctoral students and female graduates. Universities have placed higher value on external research funds, which now contribute more to their operating costs. They have pressured academics to apply for external research funds, but granting agencies typically prefer the kind of large-scale quantitative projects more often carried out by senior men.

Although effective management remains crucial to all universities, more administrative decisions are now made by professional managers rather than those drawn from the ranks of academia. In studies of university restructuring, scholars tend to criticize the rise of the managerial and corporate university, which they see as interfering with time-management, scholarship, research productivity, and academic freedom. Most seem to believe that they are working harder with less institutional recognition and support. However, men are more likely than women to accept the strengthened emphasis on research and international competitiveness and the long-hours culture. They also appear more confident that they can produce high-quality scholarly work that will be accepted and praised by their colleagues, and that they will therefore reach the top of their profession (Currie, Thiele, and Harris 2002; Fletcher et al. 2007; Probert 2005).

The academic gender gap has been diminishing for decades, yet it is nonetheless perpetuated by institutional priorities, academic practices, collegial relations, variations in family circumstances, and gendered priorities. Despite major educational, social, and institutional changes, men are still more likely than women to work in departments with a stronger research culture, to receive informal mentoring early in their career, to marry a supportive spouse who takes on most of the household chores, to view themselves as experts, and to receive acknowledgment and recognition for their research and scholarship from editors, publishers, managers, colleagues, and family members.

Many universities have already developed formal equity programs for hiring and promotion, gender-specific mentoring programs, and family-related employment leave. These programs appear to have helped more women attain academic jobs and gain promotion. However, creating a level playing field remains challenging because the work and family lives of many academics continue to be gendered, and the preferred activities of male scholars are typically granted greater professional rewards. As universities focus more on their research capacities and reputations, they tend to reinforce the advantage of those academics with the opportunity to single-mindedly pursue research interests that gain collegial recognition. This pattern suggests that the gender gap will persist even as the numbers of female academics increase. Nevertheless, it must be acknowledged that the gap has already diminished considerably over the past four decades. This implies that further improvements will continue into the future but perhaps at a slower pace than some women expected in the 1970s.

Methodological Appendix

This book is based on a survey of the existing statistics and research in the liberal states and on two of my own studies, both of which were grounded in qualitative interviews. One study was done in a Western Canadian university in 1973 and the other in two New Zealand universities in 2008. Empirical research from these two countries and decades can provide useful information about enduring or changing academic practices, gender relations at work and at home, and broader social influences on academic work. My interviews are not intended to provide a systematic comparison of the academic gender gap in Canada and New Zealand. Instead, they are used in conjunction with other studies to permit a fuller understanding of the personal experiences and perceptions of individual academics. The interviews help to illustrate the extent of social change but also the persistent academic practices and gender relations that cross national and institutional boundaries.

Both studies involved samples of participants at various ranks in the university academic hierarchy. The 1973 study included only women, whereas the 2008 one compared men and women. Both sets of interviews focused on the impact of gender and family on academic work, but their central questions varied slightly. Because the studies were not based on random samples and did not ask identical questions, the results cannot be used for systematic comparisons or be generalized to larger populations. Nevertheless, they can provide a rich understanding of participants' perceptions of university work and the impact of gender and family on career. Combined with other statistics and studies, the interviews can help us understand how and why the academic gender gap is perpetuated in the liberal states, by providing personal details from the lives of academics.

Overview of the 1973 Study

The first study, initially supervised by the late Arthur K. Davis and then by Rosalind Sydie, was done in 1973-74 at the University of Alberta (Baker 1975). It was grounded in the early analysis of the sociology of gender and work, academic practices in North American universities, and minority group theory, which I applied to women in the academic profession.

The empirical portion of the study consisted of qualitative interviews with thirty-nine women working in male-dominated departments of a large urban university in western Canada. The participants were full-time academics, temporary lecturers, and doctoral students; some doctoral students who had recently withdrawn from the program were also included in order to understand their reasons for leaving their studies at the university. Potential participants were found from the university calendar for 1973-74, from a list of academic women provided by the Academic Women's Association, and from the dean of women (in the case of doctoral students and former doctoral students). Only departments that had more than 60 percent men were sampled, but this included almost all the university's departments at the time. The study also entailed a careful reading of the university's academic handbook, manual of administrative procedures and policies, and professional ethics and standards of the Canadian Association of University Teachers. Participant observation formed part of the research, as I was a doctoral student, a temporary lecturer, a member of several departmental committees, a person with previous work experience in government (as an example of another professional job), and an applicant for several academic teaching positions.

I initially contacted the participants by telephone to make an appointment to interview them in their university offices. The semi-structured interview schedule included questions relating to educational background, career history, academic productivity and teaching load, family circumstances, career satisfaction, workplace practices, and work-life balance. The project attempted to understand how these women defined and described their professional roles, their perception of who had the power to control their careers, whether or not they thought their careers were atypical, and if they believed that women were a disadvantaged group in academia. The project also focused on the inconsistencies between the university rhetoric of academic merit and the realities of particularism experienced by the subjects.

Material from the university documents was also noted, and patterns were sought in the comments of participants: I looked for variations by university rank, discipline, age, and marital and parental status. Verbatim comments were collected from the participants to illustrate the themes that were found in the interviews and in other North American studies on the gender gap.

Overview of the 2008 Study

In 2008, thirty PhDs were interviewed at two large urban universities in New Zealand to investigate their perceptions of how gender and family circumstances affected academic careers. I have argued throughout this book that academic practices and gendered patterns in New Zealand are similar to those in Canada and the other liberal states. New Zealand universities, which rely on the international recruitment of academic staff and students, inter-university benchmarking, and national and international prestige rankings, share many of the same priorities as public universities in the other countries. Many scholars working in the two New Zealand universities were born overseas or obtained doctoral degrees and job experience outside the country, usually in the other liberal states.

The point of choosing two universities was to explore the impact of differing work environments on academics with similar qualifications. The universities differed in several respects. One stressed its research strengths and had a higher international and national ranking according to the Times Higher Education–QS World University Ranking System and New Zealand's Performance-Based Research Fund, both discussed in Chapter 3. The other university was newer, emphasized its teaching and learning capabilities, had higher teaching loads, and had slightly more females in senior ranks (New Zealand Human Rights Commission 2008).

After I received university ethics approval, potential participants were selected from the universities' websites in the humanities and social sciences. These fields were chosen because they are more gender balanced and because they limited disciplinary variations in work practices. An e-mailed invitation on University of Auckland letterhead was sent to possible candidates, containing a personally addressed letter about the study and a consent form. Despite initial intentions, the sample became heavily weighted to the research university because too few staff met the sampling criteria in the teaching university's designated schools.

The 2008 study interviewed only those academics in permanent positions (equivalent to tenure-stream or tenured in North America), even though a larger gender gap exists between temporary and permanent academics. This focus permitted an examination of the choices and constraints of those scholars whom colleagues and university managers see as the most ambitious and successful. The sample included men and women with doctorates and permanent positions at each rank of lecturer, senior lecturer, associate professor, and professor. The final sample consisted of thirty people: twenty were from the research university and ten came from the teaching university; eighteen were female and twelve were male, which constituted a response rate of about 73 percent. Some potential interviewees replied that they would have participated had they not been on sabbatical, and these were not included in the refusal rate. Only those who declined to take part or simply failed to answer my e-mail were included in the response rate.

I completed most of the interviews myself, but eight were done by Christine Todd, then a sociology master's student at the University of Auckland. All interviews, which were digitally recorded and transcribed, asked about participants' academic credentials, mentoring experiences, domestic circumstances and division of labour, perceptions of promotional opportunities, commitment to the profession, and job satisfaction. Some questions were open-ended, involving prolonged discussions of the subject's career history, whereas others asked for explicit information about family circumstances (such as living arrangements and parental status). Before the interview schedule was created, I hired a postgraduate sociology student at the University of Auckland (Helen Cox) to assist with an extensive survey of the international literature on gender and academia.

As a senior academic with some knowledge of both universities and a long academic career in four of the five liberal states, I did most of the 2008 interviews, listened to the recordings, and read and reread the transcripts, discussing some with the other interviewer. In total, we interviewed eight lecturers, eleven senior lecturers, four associate professors, and seven professors. The subjects varied from staff in their first year of post-doctoral teaching to academics near retirement; the age of the women ranged from thirty-four to sixty-two and that of the men from twenty-eight to sixty-eight. To protect their anonymity, I have omitted or disguised many personal details in discussing their comments. Furthermore, the lecturers and senior lecturers were often grouped together as junior or intermediate positions, whereas the associate professors and professors are labelled as "senior."

For the analysis, I categorized the participants' sex and age, place and date of highest degree, academic rank, type of university, and marital and parental status in a large table, and in the same table, I provided a condensed version of their mentoring experiences, family support for their career, the division of labour at home, and their expectations of promotion to professor. These particular issues have proven to be important variables in previous studies of academics. Repeated themes or common stories were extracted, and evocative verbatim comments were collated in another document to illustrate these themes. Patterns in the answers according to gender, rank, and university affiliation were noted.

Conclusion

This book is underpinned by an extensive review of the research from the liberal states about patterns of tertiary education, gendered work, family life, university restructuring, and the academic gender gap. Because both of my own studies used relatively small purposive samples,

I have been careful to make no generalizations about the larger population of academics. However, my interview findings tend to reinforce those of other studies, suggesting that the academic gender gap cuts across national and institutional boundaries.

Notes

Chapter 1: Setting the Scene

1 Evidence of the academic gender gap has been found by researchers in Australia (Asmar 1999; Bacchi 1993; Boreham et al. 2008; Carrington and Pratt 2003; Probert 2005; White 2004; Wyn, Acker, and Richards 2000), Canada (CAUT 2008a, 2008b, 2009, 2010; Drakich and Stewart 2007; Nakhaie 2007; Side and Robbins 2007), New Zealand (Ashcroft 2005; Baker 2010a, 2010c; Brooks 1997; Middleton 2009; Vasil 1993; M. Wilson 1986), the United Kingdom (Brooks 1997; Fletcher et al. 2007; Knights and Richards 2003), and the United States (AAUP 2006; Bassett 2005; Bernard 1964; Curtis 2005; Monroe et al. 2008; Sagaria 2007; Sax 2008; Toutkoushian, Bellas, and Moore 2007), to mention only a few of the many studies on this topic.

2 For a discussion of the other factors, see, for example, Henry and Tator (2009) and Kobayashi (2002).

3 Both these terms refer to scholars working in career-oriented teaching and research positions in universities. "Academic staff" is most common in Australia, New Zealand, and the United Kingdom, whereas "faculty" is typically used in North America.

4 Some academics are hired on teaching-only contracts, whereas others are hired only to do research.

5 For example, this approach was been used by Baker (2001, 2006); Baker and Tippin (1999); Bashevkin (2002); Bolderson and Mabbett (1991); Kamerman and Kahn (1997); and O'Connor, Orloff, and Shaver (1999), to name a few.

6 In comparative statistics, "senior" is defined as full professor in North America and as associate professor and professor elsewhere.

7 Considerable research also suggests that the chilly climate affects visible minorities (racial and ethnic), as well as those with working-class mannerisms and backgrounds.

8 In the past, some colleges and universities in Australia were "closed shops," which meant that academics were forced to join the union once they accepted their jobs. This is no longer the case in Australia.

9 Individual contracts were offered to academics in the New Zealand research university where the 2008 interviews were conducted.

10 In some professional schools (such as law, business, and social work), a master's degree might still be acceptable, but a doctorate would be more significant in faculties such as science or arts.

11 Tenured positions are not always permanent for life but can be abolished for a number of reasons, including the university's serious financial constraints, dwindling student numbers in the area of specialization, and serious misbehaviour of academics (called "moral turpitude" in the past).

12 Using the term "head" of department (rather than chair of department) implies a greater level of managerial authority; terminology varies by institution and jurisdiction.

13 For example, see Brenneis, Shore, and Wright (2005); Brooks and Mackinnon (2001); Butterworth and Tarling (1994); Chan and Fisher (2008); Currie, Thiele, and Harris (2002); Fisher et al. (2009); Fletcher et al. (2007); Geiger (2004); Harding (2002); Larner and LeHeron (2005); Marginson and Considine (2000); Mohrman, Ma, and Baker (2008); Schuster and Finkelstein (2006); and Slaughter and Leslie (1999).

14 New Zealand is officially bicultural but not bilingual, as Canada is. The legal system in French Canada differs to some extent from that of the rest of Canada and New Zealand.

15 I stopped interviewing at thirty-nine women because no new themes were arising in the interviews.

16 Several influential feminist books date to this period, such as Betty Friedan's *The Feminine Mystique* in 1963, Kate Millet's *Sexual Politics* in 1970, and Germaine Greer's *The Female Eunuch* in 1970.

17 In 1973, I had intended to compare men and women, but my supervisory committee insisted that I focus solely on women.

18 A growing percentage of students in these two universities are Polynesian or from various Asian countries, but most academics are white. Christine Todd, a mature master's graduate, completed about a quarter of the interviews, and I did the rest.

19 Departmental culture in the sciences, engineering, and medical fields differs notably from that in the humanities, social sciences, and education, where more women faculty are located. For example, science faculty experience stronger expectations that their research will be team-based and funded by external grants. Research teams may include colleagues but also doctoral students and postdoctoral

fellows, and are often more hierarchical than teams in the social sciences. In the sciences, resulting publications often involve shorter and joint-authored journal articles, whereas more sole-authored books and book chapters are published in the humanities and social sciences from grants.

Chapter 2: Gendered Patterns of Education, Work, and Family Life

1 At the national level, the UK statistics record "advanced" or "postgraduate" research degrees but do not separate doctoral from master's degrees.

Chapter 3: University Restructuring and Global Markets

1 The gross domestic product measures the value of all goods and services produced for pay within a country.
2 Because universities have accepted so many part-time students, they need a common measure to determine how many students they actually have, which is often calculated on a full-time basis.
3 For more details about PBRF, see the government website www.tec.govt.nz/pbrf.
4 More information about this system can be obtained from the QS University Rankings website at www.topuniversities.com.

Chapter 4: Social Capital and Gendered Responses to University Practices

1 In Australia, Canada, and New Zealand, many US and UK universities are considered more prestigious than even the best local ones. In New Zealand, this preference is sometimes labelled "colonial cringe."
2 New Zealand universities tend to pay 100 percent of salary during sabbatical leave plus a travel grant, but travel is expensive. New Zealand academics often fly to the United Kingdom, Europe, or North America for conferences and sabbaticals, which in 2008 would have cost at least $2,800 (New Zealand dollars) for one adult return airfare.
3 The travel grant at the research university is worth between $9,000 and $12,000 depending on academic rank (higher amounts for lower ranks), recognizing the high cost of travel.
4 At the research university, human resources guidelines stipulate that academics should allocate their time in the following way: 40 percent on teaching, 40 percent on research, and 20 percent on service/administration.

Chapter 7: Explaining the Academic Gender Gap

1 Teaching includes preparing and delivering lectures, leading discussion/tutorial groups or seminars, supervising postgraduate student projects, and meeting with students about their academic work, their challenges, and their future ventures.
2 Research on same-sex couples suggests a more egalitarian division of labour (Dunne 1997; Nelson 1996).

References

AAUP (Association of American University Professors). 2006. *AAUP Faculty Gender Equity Indicators 2006.* Washington, DC: AAUP.

–. 2010. *The Status of Non-Tenure-Track Faculty.* Washington, DC: AAUP.

Acker, S., and C. Armenti. 2004. "Sleepless in Academia." *Gender and Education* 16, 1: 3-24.

Acker, S., and G. Feuerverger. 1996. "Doing Good and Feeling Bad: The Work of Women University Teachers." *Cambridge Journal of Education* 26, 3: 401-22.

Acker, S., and M. Webber. 2006. "Women Working in Academe: Approach with Care." In *Handbook of Gender and Education,* ed. C. Skelton, B. Francis, and L. Smulyan, 483-96. London: Sage.

Acker, Sandra. 2003. "The Concerns of Canadian Women Academics: Will Faculty Shortages Make Things Better or Worse?" *McGill Journal of Education* 38, 3: 391-405.

–. 2010. "Gendered Games in Academic Leadership." *International Studies in the Sociology of Education* 20, 2: 129-52.

Aisenberg, Nadya, and Mona Harrington. 1988. *Women in Academe: Outsiders in the Sacred Grove.* Amherst: University of Massachusetts Press.

Alvesson, Mats, and Yvonne Due Billing. 2009. *Understanding Gender and Organizations.* London: Sage.

Ambert, Anne-Marie. 2005. "Cohabitation and Marriage: How Are They Related?" Contemporary Family Trends Series. Vanier Institute of the Family. http://www.vifamily.ca.

Armenti, Carmen. 2004. "Women Faculty Seeking Tenure and Parenthood: Lessons from Previous Generations." *Cambridge Journal of Education* 34, 1: 65-83.

Armstrong, Pat, and Hugh Armstrong. 2004. "Thinking It Through: Women, Work and Caring in the New Millennium." In *Caring For/Caring About: Women, Home Care and Unpaid Caregiving*, ed. Karen R. Grant, Carol Amaratunga, Pat Armstrong, Madeline Boscoe, Ann Pederson, and Kay Willson, 5-43. Toronto: University of Toronto Press.

–. 2010. *The Double Ghetto: Canadian Women and Their Segregated Work*. Toronto: Oxford University Press.

Ashcroft, C. 2005. "Performance Based Research Funding: A Mechanism to Allocate Funds or a Tool for Academic Promotion?" *New Zealand Journal of Educational Studies* 40, 1-2: 113-29.

Asmar, C. 1999. "Is There a Gendered Agenda in Academia? The Research Experience of Female and Male PhD Graduates in Australian Universities." *Higher Education* 38, 3: 255-73.

Astin, H.S., and J.F. Milem. 1997. "The Status of Academic Couples in U.S. Institutions." In *Academic Couples: Problems and Promises*, ed. M.A. Ferber and J.W. Loeb, 128-55. Urbana: University of Illinois Press.

Auriol, Laudeline. 2007. *Labour Market Characteristics and International Mobility of Doctorate Holders: Results for Seven Countries*. Science, Technology and Industry Working Paper 2007/2. Paris: OECD Publishing.

–. 2010. *Careers of Doctorate Holders: Employment and Mobility Patterns*. Science, Technology and Industry Working Paper 2010/04. Paris: OECD Publishing.

Australian Government. 2009. *Women in Australia 2009*. Canberra: Department of Families, Housing, Community Services and Indigenous Affairs.

Bacchi, Carol. 1993. "The Brick Wall: Why So Few Women Become Senior Academics." *Australian Universities Review* 36, 1: 36-41.

Backhouse, Constance B. 1991. *Petticoats and Prejudice: Women and Law in Nineteenth Century Canada*. Toronto: Women's Press.

Bagilhole, B., and J. Goode. 2001. "The Contradiction of the Myth of Individual Merit, and the Reality of a Patriarchal Support System in Academic Careers." *European Journal of Women's Studies* 8, 1: 161-80.

Baker, Maureen. 1975. "Women as a Minority Group in the Academic Profession." PhD thesis, University of Alberta, Edmonton.

–. 1995. *Canadian Family Policies: Cross-National Comparisons*. Toronto: University of Toronto Press.

–. 2001. *Families, Labour and Love: Family Diversity in a Changing World*. Vancouver: UBC Press.

–. 2005. "Medically Assisted Conception: Revolutionizing Family or Perpetuating a Nuclear and Gendered Model?" *Journal of Comparative Family Studies* 36, 4: 521-44.

–. 2006. *Restructuring Family Policies: Convergences and Divergences*. Toronto: University of Toronto Press.

–. 2007. *Choices and Constraints in Family Life*. Toronto: Oxford University Press.

–. 2008. "Low-Income Mothers, Employment and Welfare Restructuring." In Lunt, O'Brien, and Stephens 2008, 69-77.

–. 2009a. "The Academic Gender Gap and University Restructuring." *Atlantis: A Women's Studies Journal* 34, 1: 37-47.

–. 2009b. "Gender, Academia and the Managerial University." *New Zealand Sociology* 24, 1: 24-48.

–. 2009c. "Working Their Way out of Poverty? Gendered Employment in Three Welfare States." In "Patterns of Change and Continuity: Understanding Current Transformations in Family Life," edited by Janine Baxter. Special issue, *Journal of Comparative Family Studies* 40, 4: 617-34.

–. 2010a. "Career Confidence and Gendered Expectations of Academic Promotion." *Journal of Sociology* 46, 3: 317-34.

–. 2010b. *Choices and Constraints in Family Life*. 2nd ed. Toronto: Oxford University Press.

–. 2010c. "Choices or Constraints? Family Responsibilities, Gender and Academic Careers." *Journal of Comparative Family Studies* 41, 1: 1-18.

–. 2010d. "Motherhood, Employment and the 'Child Penalty.'" *Women's Studies International Forum* 33: 215-24.

–. 2011a. "Key Issues in Paid Parental Leave Policy." *Policy Quarterly* 7, 3: 56-63.

–. 2011b. "The Political Economy of Child Care Policy: Contradictions in New Zealand and Canada." *Policy Quarterly* 7, 1: 39-47.

Baker, Maureen, and David Tippin. 1999. *Social Assistance and the Employability of Mothers: Restructuring Welfare States*. Toronto: University of Toronto Press.

–. 2002. "When Flexibility Meets Rigidity: Sole Mothers' Experience in the Transition from Welfare to Work." *Journal of Sociology* 38, 4: 345-60.

Bakker, Isabella, and Rachel Silvey, eds. 2008. *Beyond States and Markets: The Challenges of Social Reproduction*. London: Routledge.

Banting, K.G., and C.M. Beach, eds. 1995. *Labour Market Polarization and Social Policy Reform*. Kingston: Queen's University, School of Policy Studies.

Bashevkin, Sylvia. 2002. *Welfare Hot Buttons: Women, Work, and Social Policy Reform*. Toronto: University of Toronto Press.

Bassett, Rachel Hile, ed. 2005. *Parenting and Professing*. Nashville: Vanderbilt University Press.

Baxter, Janine, Belinda Hewitt, and Michele Haynes. 2008. "Life Course Transitions and Housework: Marriage, Parenthood and Time Spent on Housework." *Journal of Marriage and Family* 70, 2: 259-72.

Beaujot, Roderic. 2000. *Earning and Caring in Canadian Families*. Peterborough: Broadview Press.

Beck, J., and M.F.D. Young. 2005. "The Assault on the Professions and the Restructuring of Academic and Professional Identities." *British Journal of Sociology of Education* 26, 2: 183-97.

Bellas, M.L., and R.K. Toutkoushian. 1999. "Faculty Time Allocations and Research Productivity: Gender, Race and Family Effects." *Review of Higher Education* 22, 4: 367-90.

–. 2003. "The Effects of Part-Time Employment and Gender on Faculty Earnings and Satisfaction." *Journal of Higher Education* 74, 2: 172-95.

Bellas, Marcia. 1994. "Comparable Worth in Academia: The Effects on Faculty Salaries of the Sex Composition and Labor Market Conditions of Academic Disciplines." *American Sociological Review* 59, 6: 807-21.

Berberet, Jerry, Carole J. Bland, Betsy E. Brown, and Kelly R. Risbey. 2005. "Late Career Faculty Perceptions: Implications for Retirement Planning and Policy-making." *Research Dialogue* 88 (June): 1-11.

Bernard, Jessie. 1964. *Academic Women.* University Park: Pennsylvania State University Press.

–. 1982. *The Future of Marriage.* 2nd ed. New York: Bantam Books.

–. 1988. "The Inferiority Curriculum." *Psychology of Women Quarterly* 12: 261-68.

Bernstein, B. 2000. *Pedagogy, Symbolic Control and Identity: Theory, Research, Critique.* Lanham, MA: Rowman and Littlefield.

Bird, S., J. Litt, and Y. Wang. 2004. "Creating Status of Women Reports: Institutional Housekeeping as 'Women's Work.'" *National Women's Studies Association Journal* 16, 1: 194-206.

Bittman, Michael, and Jocelyn Pixley. 1997. *The Double Life of the Family: Myth, Hope and Experience.* Sydney: Allen and Unwin.

Bolderson, Helen, and Deborah Mabbett. 1991. *Social Policy and Social Security in Australia, Britain and the USA.* Aldershot: Avebury.

Boreham, P., M. Western, J. Baxter, M. Dever, and W. Laffan. 2008. "Gender Differences in Early Post PhD Employment in Australian Universities." http://www.arts.monash.edu.au/.

Bourdieu, Pierre. 1977. "Cultural Reproduction and Social Reproduction." In *Power and Ideology in Education,* ed. J. Karabel and A.H. Halsey, 487-511. New York: Oxford University Press.

–. 1986. "The Forms of Capital." In *Handbook of Theory and Research for the Sociology of Education,* ed. J. Richardson, 241-58. New York: Greenwood.

–. 1988. *Homo Academicus.* Palo Alto, CA: Stanford University Press.

Boyd, Susan B. 2003. *Child Custody, Law, and Women's Work.* Toronto: Oxford University Press.

Bracken, Susan J., Jeanie K. Allen, and Diane R. Dean, eds. 2006. *The Balancing Act: Gendered Perspectives in Faculty Roles and Work Lives.* Sterling, VA: Stylus.

Bradbury, B., and K. Norris. 2005. "Income and Separation." *Journal of Sociology* 41, 4: 425-46.

Brennan, D. 2007. "The ABC of Child Care Politics." *Australian Journal of Social Issues* 42, 2: 213-25.

Brenneis, Dennis, Cris Shore, and Susan Wright. 2005. "Getting the Measure of Academia: Universities and the Politics of Accountability." *Anthropology in Action* 12, 1: 1-10.

Brooks, A., and A. Mackinnon, eds. 2001. *Gender and the Restructured University.* Buckingham, UK: Open University Press.

Brooks, Ann. 1997. *Academic Women.* Buckingham, UK: Society for Research into Higher Education and Open University Press.

Budig, Michelle, and Paula England. 2001. "The Wage Penalty for Motherhood." *American Sociological Review* 66, 2: 204-25.

Burris, Val. 2004. "The Academic Caste System: Prestige Hierarchies in PhD Exchange Networks." *American Sociological Review* 69, 2: 239-64.

Butler, Judith. 1990. *Gender Trouble: Feminism and the Subversion of Identity.* New York: Routledge, Chapman and Hall.

Butterworth, R., and N. Tarling. 1994. *Shakeup Anyway: Government and the Universities in New Zealand in a Decade of Reform.* Auckland: Auckland University Press.

Caplow, Theodore, and Reece J. McGee. 1958. *The Academic Marketplace.* New York: Basic Books.

Carr, P.L., A.S. Ash, R.H. Friedman, L. Szalacha, R.C. Barnett, A. Palepu, and M.M. Moskowitz. 2000. "Faculty Perceptions of Gender Discrimination and Sexual Harassment in Academic Medicine." *Annals of Internal Medicine* 132, 11: 889-96.

Carrington, K., and A. Pratt. 2003. "How Far Have We Come? Gender Disparities in the Australian Higher Education System." *Current Issues Brief* 31, 2002-03 (16 June). http://www.aph.gov.au/library/pubs/cib/2002-03/03cib31.pdf.

Castles, Frances G., and Ian F. Shirley. 1996. "Labour and Social Policy: Gravediggers or Refurbishers of the Welfare State?" In *The Great Experiment: Labour Parties and Public Policy Transformation in Australia and New Zealand,* ed. F. Castles, R. Gerritsen, and J. Vowles, 88-106. Auckland: Auckland University Press.

CAUT (Canadian Association of University Teachers). 2008a. "Narrowing the Gender Gap: Women Academics in Canadian Universities." *CAUT Equity Review* 2 (March). http://www.caut.ca/uploads/EquityReview2-en.pdf.

–. 2008b. "The Tenure Gap: Women's University Appointments, 1985-2005." *CAUT Equity Review* 4 (September). http://www.caut.ca.

–. 2009. *CAUT Almanac of Post-Secondary Education 2009-2010.* Ottawa: CAUT.

–. 2010. *CAUT Almanac of Post-Secondary Education 2010-2011.* Ottawa: CAUT.

–. 2011a. *CAUT Almanac of Post-Secondary Education 2011-2012.* Ottawa: CAUT.

–. 2011b. *The Persistent Gap: Understanding Male-Female Salary Differentials amongst Canadian Academic Staff.* Ottawa: CAUT.

Chan, A.S., and D. Fisher, eds. 2008. *The Exchange University: Corporatization of Academic Culture.* Vancouver: UBC Press.

Coleman, James. 1988. "Social Capital in the Creation of Human Capital." *American Journal of Sociology* Supplement 94: S95-S120.

Comer, Debra R., and Susan Stites-Doe. 2006. "Antecedents and Consequences of Faculty Women's Academic-Parental Role Balancing." *Journal of Family and Economic Issues* 27: 495-512.

Connell, R. 1995. *Masculinities.* Sydney: Allen and Unwin.

–. 2000. *The Men and the Boys.* Sydney: Allen and Unwin.

Correll, S., S. Benard, and I. Paik. 2007. "Getting a Job: Is There a Motherhood Penalty?" *American Journal of Sociology* 112, 5: 1297-1338.

Council of Graduate Schools. 2010. *Graduate Enrollment and Degrees: 1999 to 2009.* Washington, DC: Council of Graduate Schools.

Craig, Lyn. 2006. "Parental Education, Time in Paid Work and Time with Children: An Australian Time-Diary Analysis." *British Journal of Sociology* 57, 4: 553-75.

Craig, Lyn, and Michael Bittman. 2008. "The Incremental Time Costs of Children: An Analysis of Children's Impact on Adult Time Use in Australia." *Feminist Economics* 14, 2 (April): 59-88.

Creamer, Elizabeth G. 2006. "Policies That Part: Early Career Experiences of Coworking Academic Couples." In Bracken, Allen, and Dean 2006, 73-90.

Crittenden, A. 2001. *The Price of Motherhood: Why the Most Important Job in the World Is Still the Least Valued.* New York: Metropolitan Books.

Currie, Jan, Bev Thiele, and Patricia Harris. 2002. *Gendered Universities in Global Economies: Power Careers and Sacrifices.* Lanham, MD: Lexington Books.

Curtis, Bruce, and Steve Matthewman. 2005. "The Managed University: The PBRF, Its Impacts and Staff Attitudes." *New Zealand Journal of Employment Relations* 30, 2: 1-18.

Curtis, Bruce, Suzanne Phibbs, and Zoë Meager. 2011. "Exploring the Underperformance of Female Academics in the Performance-Based Research Fund." Paper presented at the conference of the Australian Sociological Association, University of Newcastle, Newcastle, Australia, 30 November.

Curtis, John W. 2005. "Inequalities Persist for Women and Non-Tenure-Track Faculty: The Annual Report on the Economic Status of the Profession 2004-2005." *Academe* 91, 2: 20-98.

Daly, M., and K. Rake. 2003. *Gender and the Welfare State.* Cambridge: Polity Press.

Dobbie, D., and I. Robinson. 2008. "Reorganizing Higher Education in the United States and Canada: The Erosion of Tenure and the Unionization of Contingent Faculty." *Labor Studies Journal* 33: 117-40.

Doucet, Andrea. 2006. *Do Men Mother?* Toronto: University of Toronto Press.

Drakich, Janice, D.E. Smith, Penni Stewart, Bonny Fox, and A. Griffith. 1991. *Status of Women in Ontario Universities: Final Report.* Vol. 1, *Overview.* Toronto: Ministry of Colleges and Universities, Government of Ontario.

Drakich, Janice, and Penni Stewart. 2007. "Forty Years Later, How Are University Women Doing?" *Academic Matters* (February): 6-9. http://www.academicmatters.ca.

Dunne, Gillian A. 1997. *Lesbian Lifestyles: Women's Work and the Politics of Sexuality.* Basingstoke: Macmillan.

Duxbury, Linda, and Chris Higgins. 2000. *Work-Life Balance in the New Millennium: Where Are We? Where Do We Need to Go?* Ottawa: Canadian Policy Research Network.

Dykstra, Pearl A. 2006. "Off the Beaten Track: Childlessness and Social Integration in Later Life." *Research on Aging* 28: 749-67.

Easton, Brian. 2008. "The Globalisation of a Welfare State." In Lunt, O'Brien, and Stephens 2008, 19-26.

Edin, K., and L. Lein. 1997. *Making Ends Meet: How Single Mothers Survive Welfare and Low-Wage Work.* New York: Russell Sage Foundation.

Edlund, Jonas. 2007. "The Work-Family Time Squeeze: Conflicting Demands of Paid and Unpaid Work among Working Couples in 29 Countries." *International Journal of Comparative Sociology* 48, 6: 451-80.

England, Paula. 2010. "The Gender Revolution: Uneven and Stalled." *Gender and Society* 24, 2 (April): 149-66.

Epstein, Cynthia. 1971. *Woman's Place: Options and Limits in Professional Careers.* Berkeley: University of California Press.

Esping-Andersen, Gøsta. 1990. *The Three Worlds of Welfare Capitalism.* Cambridge: Polity Press.

Fairbrother, Peter, and Al Rainnie. 2006. *Globalisation, State, and Labor.* New York: Routledge.

Falks, Emma. 2010. *2009-10 Academic Staff Salary Survey. Executive Summary.* London: Association of Commonwealth Universities, December.

Fels, A. 2004. "Do Women Lack Ambition?" *Harvard Business Review* (April): 50-60.

Fenton, N. 2003. "Equality Will Not Be Achieved without the Right Resources and Laws." *Guardian Education*, 1 April, 3.

Ferber, M.A., and J.W. Loeb, eds. 1997. *Academic Couples: Problems and Promises.* Urbana: University of Illinois Press.

Fisher, Donald, Kjell Rubenson, Glen Jones, and Theresa Shanahan. 2009. "The Political Economy of Post-Secondary Education: A Comparison of British Columbia, Ontario and Québec." *Higher Education* 57: 549-66.

Fletcher, Catherine, Rebecca Boden, Julie Kent, and Julie Tinson. 2007. "Performing Women: The Gendered Dimensions of the UK New Research Economy." *Gender, Work and Organization* 14, 5 (September): 433-53.

Fox, Bonnie. 2009. *When Couples Become Parents: The Creation of Gender in the Transition to Parenthood.* Toronto: University of Toronto Press.

Fox, Mary F. 2005. "Gender, Family Characteristics, and Publication Productivity among Scientists." *Social Studies of Science* 35: 131-50.

Gatta, M., and P. Roos. 2004. "Balancing without a Net in Academia: Integrating Family and Work Lives." *Equal Opportunities International* 23, 3-4-5: 124-42.

Geiger, Roger L. 2004. *Knowledge and Money: Research Universities and the Paradox of the Marketplace*. Palo Alto, CA: Stanford University Press.

Gerdes, E.P. 2003. "Do It Your Way: Advice from Senior Academic Women." *Innovative Higher Education* 27: 253-75.

–. 2006. "Women in Higher Education since 1970: The More Things Change, the More They Stay the Same." *Advancing Women in Leadership Online Journal* 21 (Summer). http://www.advancingwomen.com/awl/awl.html.

Gerson, Kathleen. 2009. "Changing Lives, Resistant Institutions: A New Generation Negotiates Gender, Work and Family Change." *Sociological Forum* 24, 4: 735-53.

Gibson, K. Sharon. 2006. "Mentoring of Women Faculty: The Role of Organizational Politics and Culture." *Innovative Higher Education* 31, 1: 63-79.

Gill, Judith, Julie Mills, Suzanne Franzway, and Rhonda Sharp. 2003. "Childfree and Feminine: Understanding the Gender Identity of Voluntarily Childless Women." *Gender and Society* 17, 1: 122-36.

–. 2008. "'Oh you must be so clever!' High-Achieving Women, Professional Power and the Ongoing Negotiation of Workplace Identity." *Gender and Education* 20, 3 (May): 223-36.

Glazer-Raymo, Judith. 1999. *Shattering the Myths: Women in Academe*. Baltimore: Johns Hopkins University Press.

–, ed. 2008. *Unfinished Agendas: New and Continuing Gender Challenges in Higher Education*. Baltimore: Johns Hopkins University Press.

Goffman, Erving. 1959. *The Presentation of Self in Everyday Life*. Garden City, NY: Doubleday Anchor.

Grant, K.R., and J. Drakich. 2010. "The Canada Research Chairs Program: The Good, the Bad and the Ugly." *Higher Education* 59, 1: 21-42.

–. 2011. "When Women Are Equal: The Canada Research Chair Experience." *Canadian Journal of Higher Education* 41, 1: 61-73.

Gray, Matthew, Lixia Qu, and Ruth Weston. 2007. *Fertility and Family Policy in Australia*. Melbourne: Australian Institute of Family Studies.

Grummell, B., D. Devine, and K. Lynch. 2009. "The Care-Less Manager: Gender, Care and New Managerialism in Higher Education." *Gender and Education* 21, 2: 191-208.

Hagestad, Gunhild O., and Vaughn R.A. Call. 2007. "Pathways to Childlessness: A Life Course Perspective." *Journal of Social Issues* 28: 1338-61.

Hantrais, Linda. 2004. *Family Policy Matters: Responding to Family Change in Europe*. Bristol: Policy Press.

Harding, S. 2002. "The Troublesome Concept of Merit." In *Gender, Teaching and Research in Higher Education: Challenges for the Twenty-First Century*, ed. G. Howie and A. Tauchert, 248-61. Aldershot: Ashgate.

Harley, S. 2003. "Research Selectivity and Female Academics in UK Universities: From Gentleman's Club and Barrack Yard to Smart Macho?" *Gender and Education* 15, 4: 378-92.

Harper, E.P., R.G. Baldwin, B.G. Gansneder, and J.L. Chronister. 2001. "Full-Time Women Faculty off the Tenure Track: Profile and Practice." *Review of Higher Education* 24: 237-57.

Hartley, Nicole, and Angela Dobele. 2009. "Feathers in the Nest: Establishing a Supportive Environment for Women Researchers." *Australian Educational Researcher* 36, 1: 43-58.

Hays, Sharon. 1996. *The Cultural Contradictions of Motherhood*. New Haven, CT: Yale University Press.

Henry, F., and C. Tator. 2009. *Racism in the Canadian University: Demanding Social Justice, Inclusion, and Equity*. Toronto: University of Toronto Press.

Hewlett, S.A., and N. Vite León. 2002. *High-Achieving Women 2001*. New York: National Parenting Association.

Hochschild, Arlie. 1989. *The Second Shift*. New York: Avon Books.

–. 1997. *The Time Bind: When Work Becomes Home and Home Becomes Work*. New York: Metropolitan Books.

Immigration New Zealand. 2011. "What Is the Population of New Zealand?" Department of Labour, Wellington. http://www.dol.govt.nz.

Jacobs, J.A. 2004. "The Faculty Time Divide." *Sociological Forum* 9: 3-27.

Jencks, C., and D. Riesman. 1977. *The Academic Revolution*. Chicago: University of Chicago Press.

Jenson, J., and M. Sineau, eds. 2001. *Who Cares? Women's Work, Childcare, and Welfare State Design*. Toronto: University of Toronto Press.

Johnson, Jennifer A., and Megan S. Johnson. 2008. "New City Domesticity and the Tenacious Second Shift." *Journal of Family Issues* 29, 4: 487-515.

Joldersma, H. 2005. *Next Steps: Report of the Gender Equity Project, University of Calgary*. University of Calgary. http://www.ucalgary.ca.

Kalleberg, Arne L. 2011. *Good Jobs, Bad Jobs: The Rise of Polarized and Precarious Employment Systems in the United States, 1970s to 2000s*. New York: Russell Sage Foundation.

Kamerman, Sheila B., and Alfred J. Kahn, eds. 1997. *Family Change and Family Policies in Great Britain, Canada, New Zealand and the United States*. Oxford: Clarendon Press.

Kelan, Elisabeth. 2009. *Performing Gender at Work*. Basingstoke: Palgrave Macmillan.

Kimmel, M.S. 2008. *The Gendered Society*. New York: Oxford University Press.

Kingfisher, Catherine, ed. 2001. *Western Welfare in Decline: Globalization and Women's Poverty*. Philadelphia: University of Pennsylvania Press.

Kinman, Gail, and Fiona Jones. 2004. *Working to the Limit: Stress and Work-Life Balance in Academic and Academic-Related Employees in the UK*. London: Association of University Teachers.

Kitterød, Ragni H., and Silje V. Pettersen. 2006. "Making Up for Mothers' Employed Working Hours?" *Work, Employment and Society* 20, 3: 473-92.

Knights, D., and W. Richards. 2003. "Sex Discrimination in UK Academia." *Gender, Work and Organization* 10, 2: 213-38.

Kobayashi, A. 2002. "Now You See Them, How You See Them: Women of Colour in Canadian Academia." In *Ivory Towers, Feminist Issues: Selected Papers from the WIN Symposia, 2000-2001,* ed. S. Heald, 44-54. Ottawa: Humanities and Social Science Federation of Canada.

Kosoko-Lasaki, Omofolasade, Roberta E. Sonnino, and Mary Lou Voytko. 2006. "Mentoring for Women and Underrepresented Minority Faculty and Students: Experience at Two Institutions of Higher Education." *Journal of the National Medical Association* 98, 9: 1449-59.

Kreitner, Robert. 2009. *Management.* 11th ed. Boston: Houghton Mifflin Harcourt.

Lamont, M. 2009. *How Professors Think: Inside the Curious World of Academic Judgment.* Cambridge, MA: Harvard University Press.

Larner, Wendy, and Richard LeHeron. 2005. "Neo-Liberalizing Spaces and Subjectivities: Reinventing New Zealand Universities." *Organization* 12, 6: 843-62.

Le Feuvre, Nicky. 2009. "Exploring Women's Academic Careers in Cross-National Perspectives: Lessons for Equal Opportunity Policies." *Equal Opportunities International* 28, 1: 9-23.

Leahey, Erin. 2006. "Gender Differences in Productivity: Research Specialisation as a Missing Link." *Gender and Society* 20, 6: 754-80.

–. 2007. "Not by Productivity Alone: How Visibility and Specialization Contribute to Academic Earnings." *American Sociological Review* 72, 4: 533-61.

Leathwood, Carole, and Barbara Read. 2008. *Gender and the Changing Face of Higher Education: A Feminized Future?* Maidenhead, UK: Open University Press.

Lim, Shirley Geok-Lin, and Maria Herrer-Sobek, eds. 2000. *Power, Race and Gender in Academe: Strangers in the Tower?* New York: Modern Language Association of America.

Lindsay, Colin. 2008. *Are Women Spending More Time on Unpaid Domestic Work than Men in Canada?* Statistics Canada Matter of Fact Series 89-630-X. Ottawa: Statistics Canada.

Lipsett, Anthea. 2008. "More Female Academics Working in Universities." *Education Guardian,* 28 February. http://www.guardian.co.uk/.

Loeb, J.W. 2001. "The Role of Recognition and Reward in Research Productivity: Implications for Partner Collaboration." In *Working Equal: Academic Couples as Collaborators,* ed. Elizabeth G. Creamer, 167-85. New York: Routledge-Falmer.

Long, J. 2001. *From Scarcity to Visibility.* Washington, DC: National Academic Press.

Long, J., and M.F. Fox. 1995. "Scientific Careers: Universalism and Particularism." *Annual Review of Sociology* 21: 45-71.

Lucas, L. 2006. *The Research Game in Academic Life.* Maidenhead: Open University Press.

Luke, C. 1997. "Quality Assurance and Women in Higher Education." *Higher Education* 33, 4: 433-51.

Lunt, N., M. O'Brien, and R. Stephens, eds. 2008. *New Zealand, New Welfare.* Melbourne: CENGAGE Learning.

Lunt, Neil. 2008. "New Measures to Reduce Sickness and Invalids Benefits Rolls." In Lunt, O'Brien, and Stephens 2008, 92-100.

Luxton, M. 2006. "Feminist Political Economy in Canada and the Politics of Social Reproduction." In *Social Reproduction: Feminist Political Economy Challenges Neo-Liberalism,* ed. K. Bezanson and M. Luxton, 11-44. Montreal and Kingston: McGill-Queen's University Press.

Lynch, Karen D. 2008. "Gender Roles and the American Academe: A Case Study of Graduate Student Mothers." *Gender and Education* 20, 6: 585-605.

MacDonald, Martha. 2009. "Income Security for Women: What About Employment Insurance?" In *Public Policy for Women,* ed. M. Cohen and J. Pulkingham, 251-70. Toronto: University of Toronto Press.

Malcolm, J., and M. Zukas. 2009. "Making a Mess of Academic Work: Experience, Purpose, Identity." *Teaching in Higher Education* 14, 5: 495-506.

Marginson, Simon, and Mark Considine. 2000. *The Enterprise University: Power, Governance and Reinvention in Australia.* Cambridge: Cambridge University Press.

Mason, M.A., and Marc Goulden. 2002. "Do Babies Matter? The Effect of Family Formation on the Lifelong Careers of Academic Men and Women." *Academe* 88, 6: 21-28.

–. 2004. "Marriage and Baby Blues: Redefining Gender Equity in the Academy." *Annals of the American Academy of Political and Social Science* 596: 86-103.

Mason, Mary Ann, Marc Goulden, and Nicholas H. Wolfinger. 2006. "Babies Matter: Pushing the Gender Equity Revolution Forward." In Bracken, Allen, and Dean 2006, 9-28.

McMahon, Anthony. 1999. *Taking Care of Men: Sexual Politics in the Public Mind.* Melbourne: Cambridge University Press.

Menzies, Heather, and Janice Newson. 2008. "Time, Stress and Intellectual Engagement in Academic Work: Exploring Gender Difference." *Gender, Work and Organization* 15, 5 (September): 504-22.

Metcalfe, A.S. 2010. "Revisiting Academic Capitalism in Canada: No Longer the Exception." *Journal of Higher Education* 81, 4: 489-514.

Middleton, Sue. 2009. "Becoming PBRF-able." In *Assessing the Quality of Educational Research in Higher Education,* ed. Tina Besley, 193-208. Rotterdam: Sense.

Mohrman, Kathryn, Wanhua Ma, and David Baker. 2008. "The Research University in Transition: The Emerging Global Modal." *Higher Education Policy* 21: 5-27.

Monroe K., S. Ozyurt, T. Wrigley, and A. Alexander. 2008. "Gender Equality in Academia: Bad News from the Trenches, and Some Possible Solutions." *Perspectives on Politics* 6, 2: 215-33.

Moore, Gwen. 1988. "Women in Elite Positions: Insiders or Outsiders?" *Sociological Forum* 3, 4: 566-95.

Morley, Louise. 2003. *Quality and Power in Higher Education.* Maidenhead, UK, and Philadelphia: Open University Press and Society for Research into Higher Education.

Moyer, A., P. Salovey, and S. Casey-Cannon. 1999. "Challenges Facing Female Doctoral Students and Recent Graduates." *Psychology of Women Quarterly* 23: 607-30.

Muzzin, L., and J. Limoges. 2008. "'A Pretty Incredible Structural Injustice': Contingent Faculty in Canadian University Nursing." In Wagner, Acker, and Mayuzumi 2008, 157-72.

Nakhaie, M. Reza. 2002. "Gender Differences in Publication among University Professors in Canada." *Canadian Review of Sociology and Anthropology* 39, 2: 151-80.

–. 2007. "Universalism, Ascription and Academic Rank: Canadian Professors, 1987-2000." *Canadian Review of Sociology and Anthropology* 44, 3: 361-86.

Nayak, Anoop, and Mary Jane Kehily. 2008. *Gender, Youth and Culture: Young Masculinities and Femininities.* Basingstoke, UK: Palgrave Macmillan.

Nelson, F. 1996. *Lesbian Motherhood.* Toronto: University of Toronto Press.

New Zealand Human Rights Commission. 2008. *New Zealand Census of Women's Participation.* Wellington. http://www.neon.org.nz.

New Zealand Ministry of Education. 2009. "Statistics: Tertiary Education; Gaining Qualifications." In *Education Counts.* Wellington, Government of New Zealand. http://www.educationcounts.govt.nz.

NZVC (New Zealand Vice-Chancellor's Committee). 2010. "The New Zealand University System." http://www.nzvcc.ac.nz.

O'Connor, Julia S., Ann Shola Orloff, and Sheila Shaver. 1999. *States, Markets, Families: Gender Liberalism and Social Policy in Australia, Canada, Great Britain and the United States.* Cambridge: Cambridge University Press.

OECD (Organisation for Economic Co-operation and Development). 2002. *OECD Employment Outlook July 2002.* Paris: OECD.

–. 2007a. *Babies and Bosses: Reconciling Work and Family Life.* Vol. 5, *A Synthesis of Findings for OECD Countries.* Paris: OECD. http://www.oecd.org/.

–. 2007b. *Society at a Glance: OECD Social Indicators 2006.* Paris: OECD.

–. 2008a. *Employment Outlook 2008.* Paris: OECD.

–. 2008b. *Growing Unequal? Income Distribution and Poverty in OECD Countries.* Paris: OECD.

–. 2009a. *Highlights from Education at a Glance 2009.* Paris: OECD.

–. 2009b. *OECD Employment Outlook 2009: Tackling the Job Crisis.* Paris: OECD.

–. 2009c. *Society at a Glance: OECD Social Indicators 2009.* Paris: OECD.

O'Laughlin, E.M., and L.G. Bischoff. 2005. "Balancing Parenthood and Academia: Work/Family Stress as Influenced by Gender and Tenure Status." *Journal of Family Issues* 26: 79-106.

Ornstein, M., P. Stewart, and J. Drakich. 2007. "Promotion at Canadian Universities: The Intersection of Gender, Discipline and Institution." *Canadian Journal of Higher Education* 37, 3: 1-25.

Patterson, Michelle. 1971. "Alice in Wonderland: A Study of Women Faculty in Graduate Departments of Sociology." *American Sociologist* 6 (August): 226-34.

Peters, M., and P. Roberts. 1999. *University Futures and the Politics of Reform in New Zealand.* Dunedin: Dunmore Press.

Pettit, Becky, and Jennifer L. Hook. 2009. *Gendered Tradeoffs: Family, Social Policy and Economic Inequality in Twenty-One Countries.* New York: Russell Sage Foundation.

Portanti, Martina, and Simon Whitworth. 2009. *A Comparison of the Characteristics of Childless Women and Mothers in the ONS Longitudinal Study.* London: Office for National Statistics.

Potuchek, J.L. 1997. *Who Supports the Family: Gender and Breadwinning in Dual-Earner Marriages.* Stanford, CA: Stanford University Press.

Probert, Belinda. 2005. "'I Just Couldn't Fit It In': Gender and Unequal Outcomes in Academic Careers." *Gender, Work and Organization* 12, 1: 50-72.

Putnam, Robert D. 2000. *Bowling Alone: The Collapse and Revival of American Community.* New York: Simon and Schuster.

Qu, Lixia, and Ruth Weston. 2008. "Snapshot of Family Relationships." *Family Matters* (May). http://www.aifs.gov.au.

Ransley, James. 2007. "Patriarchy Dominates PBRF System." *Salient* (Victoria University of Wellington), 23 July. http://salient.org.nz.

Ranson, Gillian. 2009. "Paid and Unpaid Work: How Do Families Divide Their Labour?" In *Families: Changing Trends in Canada*, 6th ed., ed. M. Baker, 108-29. Toronto: McGraw-Hill Ryerson.

Reay, D., J. Davies, M. David, and S.J. Ball. 2001. "Choices of Degrees or Degrees of Choice? Class, 'Race' and the Higher Education Choice Process." *Sociology* 35: 855-77.

Reimer, M., ed. 2004. *Inside Corporate U: Women in the Academy Speak Out.* Toronto: Sumach Press.

Rhoades, Gary. 1998. *Managed Professionals: Unionized Faculty and Restructuring Academic Labor.* Albany: State University of New York Press.

Robbins, Wendy, Meg Luxton, Margrit Eichler, and Francine Descarries. 2008. *Minds of Our Own: Inventing Feminist Scholarship and Women's Studies in Canada and Québec, 1966-76.* Waterloo: Wilfrid Laurier Press.

Rosser, S.V. 2004. "Using POWRE to ADVANCE: Institutional Barriers Identified by Women Scientists and Engineers." *NWSA Journal* 16, 1: 50-78.

Rossiter, M.W. 1993. "The Matilda Effect in Science." *Social Studies of Science* 23, 2: 325-41.

Rothstein, Richard. 2004. *Social Class and Schools: Using Social, Economic and Educational Reform to Close the Black-White Achievement Gap.* New York: Columbia University Press.

Royal Commission on the Status of Women in Canada. 1970. *Report*. Ottawa: Supply and Services Canada.

Sagaria, Mary Ann Danovitz, ed. 2007. *Women, Universities and Change: Gender Equality in the European Union and the United States*. Basingstoke: Palgrave Macmillan.

Sax, Linda. 2008. *The Gender Gap in College: Maximizing the Development Potential of Men and Women*. San Francisco: Jossey-Bass Higher and Adult Education.

Schuster, Jack H., and Martin J. Finkelstein. 2006. *The American Faculty: The Restructuring of Academic Work and Careers: Who We Are*. Baltimore: Johns Hopkins University Press.

Scruggs, Lyle, and James Allan. 2006. "Welfare State De-Commodification in 18 Welfare States." *European Journal of Social Policy* 16, 1: 55-72.

Seagram, B.C., J. Gould, and S. Pyke. 1998. "An Investigation of Gender and Other Variables on Time to Completion of Doctoral Degrees." *Research in Higher Education* 39, 3: 319-35.

Settles, I., L.M. Cortina, J. Malley, and A.J. Stewart. 2006. "The Climate for Women in Academic Science: The Good, the Bad, and the Changeable." *Psychology of Women Quarterly* 30: 47-58.

Side, Katherine, and Wendy Robbins. 2007. "Institutionalizing Inequalities in Canadian Universities: The Canada Research Chairs Program." In "Women, Tenure, and Promotion." Special issue *NWSA Journal* 19, 3: 163-81.

Sikes, P. 2006. "Working in a 'New' University: In the Shadow of the Research Assessment Exercise?" *Studies in Higher Education* 31, 5: 555-68.

Slaughter, Sheila, and Larry L. Leslie. 1999. *Academic Capitalism*. Baltimore: Johns Hopkins University Press.

Statistics Canada. 2008. "Age at Retirement, by Sex." *The Canadian Labour Market at a Glance* 71-222-X. http://www.statcan.gc.ca.

–. 2009. *Graduating in Canada: Profile, Labour Market Outcomes and Student Debt of the Class of 2005*. Catalogue 81-595. Ottawa: Statistics Canada.

–. 2011. "Canada's Population Estimates." *The Daily*, 24 March. http://www.statcan.gc.ca.

Stephens, R., and P. Callister. 2008. "Work-Life Balance." In Lunt, O'Brien, and Stephens 2008, 125-36.

Sussman, Deborah, and Lahouaria Yssaad. 2005. "The Rising Profile of Women Academics." *Perspectives* 6, 2 (February): 6-19.

Sweet, S., and P. Moen. 2002. *Intimate Academics: Co-Working Couples in Two American Universities*. Working Paper BLCC 02-23. Ithaca, NY: Cornell University, Cornell Careers Institute.

Tahir, Tariq. 2010. "The Irresistible Rise of Academic Bureaucracy." *The Guardian*, 30 March. http://www.guardian.co.uk.

Taylor, P., and R. Braddock. 2007. "International University Ranking Systems and the Idea of University Excellence." *Journal of Higher Education Policy and Management* 29, 3: 245-60.

Thomas, Robyn, and Annette Davies. 2002. "Gender and New Public Management: Reconstituting Academic Subjectivities." *Gender, Work and Organization* 9, 4: 372-97.

Tizard, Barbara, and Charlie Owen. 2001. "Activities and Attitudes of Retired University Staff." *Oxford Review of Education* 27, 2: 253-70.

Torjman, Sherri, and Ken Battle. 1999. *Good Work: Getting It and Keeping It.* Ottawa: Caledon Institute of Social Policy.

Toutkoushian, R.K., M.L. Bellas, and J.V. Moore. 2007. "The Interaction Effects of Gender, Race, and Marital Status on Faculty Salaries." *Journal of Higher Education* 78, 5: 572-601.

Turk, James. 2000. *The Corporate Campus: Commercialization and the Dangers to Canada's Colleges and Universities.* Toronto: James Lorimer.

United Kingdom National Statistics. 2008. *Higher Education, Skills and Qualifications, 2008.* London: UK Government.

University of Auckland, Equal Employment Opportunities Office. 2006. *Annual Summary of Statistics 2006.* Auckland: University of Auckland, Equal Employment Opportunities Office.

–. 2010. *Equity 2010: Statistics and Activities.* Auckland: University of Auckland, Equal Employment Opportunities Office.

Valian, V. 1998. *Why So Slow? The Advancement of Women.* Cambridge, MA: MIT Press.

–. 2004. "Beyond Gender Schemas: Improving the Advancement of Women in Academia." *National Women's Studies Association Journal* 16, 1: 207-20.

Van De Werfhorst, Herman G., Alice Sullivan, and Sin Yi Cheung. 2003. "Social Class, Ability and Choice of Subject in Secondary and Tertiary Education in Britain." *British Educational Research Journal* 29, 1: 41-62.

van Emmerik, I.J. Hetty. 2006. "Gender Differences in the Creation of Different Types of Social Capital: A Multilevel Study." *Social Networks* 28: 24-37.

Vasil, L. 1993. "Gender Differences in the Academic Career in New Zealand Universities." *New Zealand Journal of Educational Studies* 28, 2: 143-63.

VIF (Vanier Institute of the Family). 2008. "Fertility Intentions: If, When and How Many?" *Fascinating Families* 13. http://www.vifamily.ca/media/node/260/attachments/ff13.pdf.

Vosko, Leah F. 2000. *Temporary Work: The Gendered Rise of a Precarious Employment Relationship.* Toronto: University of Toronto Press.

–. 2002. "The Pasts (and Futures) of Feminist Political Economy in Canada: Reviving the Debate." *Studies in Political Economy* 68 (Summer): 55-83.

–. 2009. "Precarious Employment and the Challenges for Employment Policy." In *Public Policy for Women,* ed. M. Cohen and J. Pulkingham, 374-95. Toronto: University of Toronto Press.

Vosko, Leah F., Martha MacDonald, and Iain Campbell. 2009. *Gender and the Contours of Precarious Employment.* London: Routledge.

Wagner, A., S. Acker, and K. Mayuzumi, eds. 2008. *Whose University Is It, Anyway? Power and Privilege on Gendered Terrain.* Toronto: Sumach Press.

Waisbren, Susan E., et al. 2008. "Gender Differences in Research Grant Applications and Funding Outcomes for Medical School Faculty." *Journal of Women's Health* 17, 2: 207-14.

Walby, S., H. Gottfried, K. Gottschall, and M. Osawa. 2007. *Gendering the Knowledge Economy: Comparative Perspectives.* Basingstoke: Palgrave Macmillan.

Wall, Glenda. 2009. "Childhood and Child-Rearing." In *Families: Changing Trends in Canada*, 6th ed., ed. Maureen Baker, 91-107. Toronto: McGraw-Hill Ryerson.

Walter, M. 2002. "Working Their Way Out of Poverty? Sole Motherhood, Work, Welfare and Material Well-Being." *Journal of Sociology* 38, 4 (December): 361-80.

Weedon, J., M. Abrams, M. Green, and J. Sabini. 2006. "Do High-Status People Really Have Fewer Children?" *Human Nature* 17, 4: 377-92.

West, C., and D.H. Zimmerman. 1987. "Doing Gender." *Gender and Society* 1, 2: 125-51.

West, Martha S., and John W. Curtis. 2006. *AAUP Faculty Gender Equity Indicators 2006.* Washington, DC: American Association of University Professors.

Weston, Ruth, Lixia Qu, Robyn Parker, and Michael Alexander. 2004. *'It's not for lack of wanting kids ...' A Report on the Fertility Decision Making Project.* Research Report 11. Melbourne: Australian Institute of Family Studies.

White, K. 2004. "The Leaking Pipeline: Women Postgraduate and Early Career Researchers in Australia." *Tertiary Education and Management* 10, 3: 227-41.

Wickens, Christine M. 2008. "The Organizational Impact of University Labour Unions." *Higher Education* 56, 5: 545-64.

Wilson, M. 1986. *Report on the Status of Academic Women in New Zealand.* Wellington: Association of University Staff of New Zealand.

Wilson, Marnie, Shannon Gadbois, and Kathleen Nichol. 2008. "Is Gender Parity Imminent in the Professoriate? Lessons from One Canadian University." *Canadian Journal of Education* 31, 1: 211-28.

Wilson, Sue. 2009. "Partnering, Cohabitation, and Marriage." In *Families: Changing Trends in Canada*, 6th ed., ed. Maureen Baker, 68-90. Toronto: McGraw-Hill Ryerson.

Wolfinger, Nicholas H., Mary Ann Mason, and Marc Goulden. 2008. "Problems in the Pipeline: Gender, Marriage, and Fertility in the Ivory Tower." *Journal of Higher Education* 79, 4: 388-405.

Wolfram, Hans-Joachim, Gisela Mohr, and Birgit Schyns. 2007. "Professional Respect for Female and Male Leaders: Influential Gender-Relevant Factors." *Women in Management Review* 22, 1: 19-32.

Wolf-Wendel, Lisa, S.B. Twombly, and S. Rice. 2003. *Two Body Problem: Dual-Career-Couple Hiring in Higher Education.* Baltimore: Johns Hopkins University Press.

Wu, Zheng. 2000. *Cohabitation: An Alternative Form of Family Living.* Don Mills: Oxford University Press.

Wu, Zheng, and Christoph Schimmele. 2009. "Divorce and Repartnering." In *Families: Changing Trends in Canada,* 6th ed., ed. M. Baker, 154-78. Toronto: McGraw-Hill Ryerson.

Wyn, J., S. Acker, and E. Richards. 2000. "Making a Difference: Women in Management in Australian and Canadian Faculties of Education." *Gender and Education* 12, 4: 435-38.

Xie, Y., and K.A. Shauman. 1998. "Sex Differences in Research Productivity: New Evidence about an Old Puzzle." *American Sociological Review* 63, 6: 847-70.

Zhang, X. 2009. "Earnings of Women With and Without Children." *Perspectives* 10, 3 (March): 5-13.

Index

Printed and bound in Canada by Friesens

Set in Myriad and Sabon by Artegraphica Design Co. Ltd.

Copy editor: Deborah Kerr

Proofreader: Steph Vander Meulen